RSHIP

By the same author:
Teach Yourself Praise Guitar

Leading Worship

JO KING

KINGSWAY PUBLICATIONS
EASTBOURNE

First published 1988

ISBN 0 86065 489 3

Unless otherwise indicated, biblical quotations are from the Revised Standard Version copyrighted 1946, 1952, © 1971, 1973 by the Division of Christian Education of the National Council of the Churches of Christ in the USA

NIV = New International Version
copyright © International Bible Society 1973, 1978, 1984

AV = Authorized Version
crown copyright

SOF refers to the *Integrated Songs of Fellowship* songbook.

Printed in Great Britain for
KINGSWAY PUBLICATIONS LTD
Lottbridge Drove, Eastbourne, E. Sussex BN23 6NT by
Stanley L. Hunt (Printers) Ltd, Rushden, Northants.
Typeset by Nuprint Ltd, Harpenden, Herts AL5 4SE.

CONTENTS

PART ONE: PUTTING THEORY INTO PRACTICE

PART TWO: PREPARATION FOR A MEETING

PART THREE: IN THE MEETING

ACKNOWLEDGEMENTS

To my wife, Jude, for supporting me while I wrote the book, and to Linda Harris for checking and correcting the manuscript. Also to Anne Braithwaite for help with the typing.

Please note that this book should be used in conjunction with the cassette, *Leading Worship*.

Part One

Putting Theory into Practice

I

Praise the Lord! Who?

One of the main functions of a worship leader is to point people Godward, reminding them of who God is and who he isn't. Their worship will be great or feeble according to their view of God. Let's praise the Lord, but let's be sure there are no negative images of 'Lord' inhibiting our praise.

Before a person becomes a Christian, their perception of God can be drawn from all kinds of sources. Until these wrong concepts are dealt with, they will be unable to come into a full enjoyment of the love of God, which he wants them to have. For some, God is still regarded as the headmaster figure who is distant, austere and stern. To others he is seen as the teacher who is a kill-joy, intolerant and always checking up on them—without the pass-mark they had better keep their distance. God may even be looked upon as the boss who is aloof, unapproachable and uninvolved. Their idea of God might even come from art or films. Film epics such as *The Greatest Story Ever Told* and *King of Kings*, which contain more Hollywood than Bible, depict Jesus with a face like a well-kept grave. Maybe this is what the worshipper sees when he closes his eyes and visualizes his 'Lord'. One minister told me that for years it had been an effort for him not to imagine God with a frown.

On the other hand, God may not be considered to be a harsh figure but someone who is soft, even effeminate. When I was at school, there were pictures of Jesus in the RE room which portrayed him with hair glistening in the sunlight. Some of the youngsters used to poke fun and say, 'He's wearing Harmony hairspray!' At that time I regarded Jesus as the soft spot in the Trinity, the one with whom I could get away with anything. The fact that he is as eager to forgive us as a father is eager to rescue his child from a fire, can cause us to sponge off his love, rather than be sorry enough not to do it again.

For some, the very mention of God as 'Father' can arouse painful memories of a turbulent relationship with a dad who was unfeeling, busy or uninterested. The concept of fatherhood proves difficult to others because as a youngster their father was a vague, shadowy figure whom they never really knew, due to either death or divorce.

A person coming to worship God can unconsciously superimpose any of these authority figures on him. It may not be the case to any great degree with most of us, but in some measure I believe we have all been affected.

If someone is finding worship to be a task of endurance, they may well need prayer and ministry to remove these ingrained attitudes. In such cases, the enemy will invariably have been at work, reinforcing the problem. He knows those who are more prone to digesting his lies than God's truth. Satan's first ploy with Eve was not to get her to doubt God's existence but his character. He is still using the same tactics today and he is finding the same easy prey.

Therefore, when you are leading the people to praise the Lord, *persuade them of his love for them*. Tell them that he is not intolerant of them. Even if we repeatedly bring a problem to him, he will never say, 'Oh no! Not you again!' but rather, 'What kept you?' Convince them that God never tires of our praises. We may have had the experience of talking to someone, aware that we haven't got their full concentration or interest. Thankfully, God never half-listens to us. He is fully attentive to our efforts in worship.

Encourage the people to see that they are coming to a tender-hearted Father. Of course, no one can call God 'Father' unless they know they're his child. Only the Holy Spirit can ignite this reality in us. We cannot produce a work of the Spirit with a work of the flesh. It is of little use hearing second-hand that God loves us. For example, it is no good for my wife to hear of my love for her from other people unless she primarily hears it from me. We need to hear it from God, but not just in the head—the penny has to drop eighteen inches!

In Song of Songs 1:4 we are told to come right into the inner chambers of the King. We are told not to draw near on tiptoe but 'with confidence' (Heb 4:16). As you lead worship, encourage a reception to a revelation and experience of God's love and an enjoyment of the intimate position he has called us to. There may be those present who still have a relationship with a concept of God rather than with God himself.

2

Praise the Lord! Why?

To follow the Maker's instructions

'The people I formed for myself that they might declare my praise' (Is 43:21). When something is not used for the purpose for which it was designed, malfunction will result. We were created for the purpose of worshipping God. A neglect of this basic instinct will lead to malnutrition and corruption of the human condition because we are simply not functioning as we ought.

Malnutrition

'If you don't worship, you'll shrink' (Peter Shaffner, *Equus*).

Primitive peoples used to worship things which gave them sustenance, for example, the sun, wind and rain. Today the objects of worship have changed but people still focus on things which provide fulfilment and meaning, for example, money, cars, music, sport and houses. Yet when the world inside us is dry and thirsty, nothing from the world outside us can really satisfy. One of the biggest lies perpetrated by Satan is that if you only get enough things in life, you'll be happy. However, no amount of money, fame, influence, power, respectability or knowledge can nourish the human spirit. No person, even, can satisfy another person's spiritual needs. Attempts to meet spiritual needs with material, physical or emotional substitutes are futile, even damaging. Square pegs don't fit into round holes! Worship is as essential to the spirit as food is to the body and love to the heart.

Corruption

We become like that which we worship.

God has implanted a need and desire to worship him within us. The human spirit naturally wants to make contact with God's Spirit. When this fundamental instinct for God is ignored or denied, it will find expression in other ways. If it is misdirected to other sources, they can be corrupting influences. For example:

(a) Exodus 32:7—The Israelites worship a golden calf (materialism).
(b) Matthew 20:20–21—James and John focus on a position of influence.
(c) Acts 8:18–19—Simon Magus desires spiritual power.

In each case, natural instinct was urging the people concerned to worship God, but they misdirected their worship to corrupting influences. When the human spirit is itching, only God's Spirit can scratch it.

To give him pleasure

God did not create us because he was lonely, bored, or needing something to worship him. That is selfish and God is not selfish. He created us to *share* in the community of the Father, Son and Holy Spirit.

When you are leading, help people to see that:

God is thrilled by their praises

'The Lord chose them [the Levites] to carry the ark of the Lord and *to minister to him* for ever' (1 Chron 15:2, italics mine). The idea of God being ministered to, influenced, touched and even roused by our worship, is still alien to many believers. God is not like some cosmic grandfather rocking benignly on his celestial rocking chair, unmoved by our singing. If we think he is impassive and unresponsive to us, then we've missed one of the main reasons for worshipping— to give him pleasure (Rev 4:11).

An incident from a film I once saw brought this home to me. The heroine turns to the hero and brimming over with love for him says, 'I love you!' He responds without a trace of emotion, and in a nonchalant, super-cool manner replies, 'Yes, I know.'

Thankfully, God never remains unaffected by our praises.

God enjoys being our 'big Dad'

I once heard a worship leader say that God doesn't need our praises. Though true, this kind of statement can quench people's motivation. They might well ask, 'Why do it then?' No, God doesn't *need* our praises. However, because of God's essential nature as Father, he responds to our love and praise with the same pleasure and elation a human father would feel when his children rush to his open arms to receive a cuddle from him.

God desires us to enter his throne room with a holy boldness (Eph 3:11–12)—*not* a holy brashness. Visitors to the Oval Office of President John F. Kennedy in the White House used to be surprised to find his small son playing at his feet while the President worked on matters of State at his desk. We should have this same confidence, born of sonship, to approach the throne of our heavenly Father. We are welcomed as children (see Heb 4:16; 10:19, 22). In the story of the Prodigal Son, the moment of embrace between father and son (Lk 15:20) sums up how intimate God wants us to be with him. We must not rob him or ourselves of this intimacy.

It is our destiny

When all else has ceased, worship will continue (Rev 7:9–11), so we need to get practising!

3

Praise the Lord! When?

Now

Worship is a response to God and he is accessible in any place and at any time and that means *now*. 'Now is the acceptable time . . .' (2 Cor 6:2). We must not think, 'I'll pray later when I have more time. I'm in a bit of a rush now and I've only got a few minutes.' If we're not able to use one minute properly, we're unlikely to use one hour properly. 'The hour . . . now is, when the true worshippers will worship the Father' (Jn 4:23).

Always

A helpful way of determining whether you are the kind of true worshipper Jesus was talking about in John 4:23, is to look at the use of the word 'worship' in everyday life. We say of someone that they worship their team, car, money, house or boyfriend because they have passed beyond the point of simply being interested to a more intense state of preoccupation.

For example, a fan of a rock star will travel any distance, queue for any length of time and spend any sum of money to see the object of his worship. His idol will occupy most of his thoughts and be one of his favourite topics of conversation.

Tozer has said, 'Christians are called to an everlasting preoccupation with God.' Worship is a daily relationship, not a weekly event. We worship only as much as we worship day by day. Some people can be devils at home and saints at church, but God is not fooled by such superficiality and deception, and warns in Amos 5:23, 'Take away from me the noise of your songs; to the melody of your harps I will not listen.'

True worship arises out of spiritual consistency.

4

Praise the Lord! How?

As we corporately express our worship to God through songs, various aspects of our being should be involved.

THE MIND

'I will sing with the spirit and I will sing with the understanding also' (1 Cor 14:15, AV). Singing, even the most exuberant type, should always be an intelligent, thoughtful act, where the mind never ceases to be active. The people should be encouraged to let everything they sing have significance. Christians don't tell many lies but they sing thousands. This is true of songs that are well-known, especially overfamiliar ones.

One of the main hindrances in worship is the wandering mind. If we forget *who* we're singing to and *what* we're singing about, it won't be long before we're thinking about rising prices, Sunday lunch and the film we saw last night. To combat this, a few words at the beginning of your time together on meaningful, thoughtful worship might help.

Songs usually fall into a number of categories:

Songs sung to God

For example, *I just want to praise You.* Worship means 'to think magnificently about God' (Professor A. J. Gossip). The word 'magnificently' here means 'make large' from which we can get the sense of 'letting your mind be stretched'. Of course, we also talk of 'magnifying God' in the sense of declaring how great he is.

Songs sung to yourself

For example, *Bless the Lord, O my soul.* In some songs the focus of attention can shift. For example, the first few lines of *I love You, Lord* are addressed to God, but they are followed by the lines, 'O my soul, rejoice.'

Songs sung to each other

For example, *Our God reigns.* Such songs can be sung with great zeal yet everyone is worshipping in their own little circle. Help people to be aware of others around them. Though worship means loving God in the presence of others, it also means loving others in the presence of God. At times it may be necessary to help people to break out of the reserve which isolates them in worship by encouraging them to hold hands, look around or move.

Songs sung against the enemy

For example, *Through our God we shall do valiantly.* If you are praying about a situation where you feel the enemy has been active, such songs can be used like tanks of praise to reinforce the guns of prayer in intercession.

When leading, there may be occasions when you sense people are lacking in concentration as they sing and are simply going through the motions. The best way of dealing with this is not to bring it to their notice, and certainly not to exercise the 'ministry of rebuke'! Saying something along the lines of: 'As we sing the next song, let's allow the Holy Spirit to minister these familiar words to us afresh,' might help.

It may also help if you encourage people to praise God for something. To illustrate this, visualize a conveyor-belt between the congregation and God. As we sing to God, it is as if we are placing a parcel on the moving belt. God is thrilled to receive what appears to be a present and begins to unwrap the ribbons and paper, only to find there is nothing inside. Songs without a heart of thoughtful praise can be like the outer wrappings of an empty parcel.

A man once had a dream. He dreamt he was standing beside God who was looking over the balconies of heaven. As they both peered through the clouds, they could see right down into the man's church. A service was in progress, and the large congregation was singing a hymn. Unfortunately, there was no sound being produced, just the motion of people's lips; that is, apart from one small boy. The man asked God why it was that only this child's praises were reaching heaven. God sadly replied, 'He is the only one who is singing from his heart.'

When you are leading singing, be aware that at times people's lips might move but their hearts might not be moved; their lips might be responding but their hearts might not be. Encourage people to be alive to God not just mentally but emotionally as well (not emotionalism which is emotion without root). If they are not singing with their mind, their emotions will remain untouched.

'I will praise you, O Lord my God, with all my heart' (Ps 86:12). See also Ps 5:11; 9:2, 14; 13:5; 16:9; 21:1; 31:7; 32:11; 33:1; 34:2; 42:4; 53:6; 71:8; 86:12; 89:16; 92:4; 95:1–2; 96:11; 97:1, 8, 12; 107:22; 118:24; 126:2; 149:2; 2 Sam 6:5.

Our well-being

It is clear from Scripture that God wants joy in his worship. Because he always has our interests at heart more than his own, the command, 'Make a joyful noise to the Lord... make a loud noise, and rejoice' (Ps 98:4, AV) is really an offer. It is we, more than God, who need to hear and see ourselves being caught up in rejoicing. God has prescribed joy for our well-being. 'A cheerful heart is a good medicine but a downcast spirit dries up the bones' (Prov 17:22). Are we taking the medicine?

The Greek for 'to sing' is 'to celebrate God in song'. Imagine that in our times of celebrating God, we are presenting him with a beautiful jam sponge. If the cake consisted mainly of jam and very little sponge, it would be rather sickly to eat. Too much sponge without adequate quantities of jam would also be difficult to swallow and digest. Very often churches have robbed themselves of the nourishment of different types of worship. Polarization has occurred because extrovert people who want loud worship go to denomination A and introvert people who want quiet worship go to denomination B. Someone has said, 'If you're all word, you dry up; if you're all spirit, you blow up, but if you're both, you grow up.' Sometimes we don't grow up and develop spiritual muscles because we're served a meagre diet of a few hymns and songs. In the past, it hasn't been so much that the church has been at fault in what it has taught, but in what it *hasn't* taught. We have majored on big issues and neglected what we thought were small issues—like worship!

His honour

God also wants joy in our worship of him because it isn't honouring to him that unbelievers should regard places of worship as joyless. It should be evident to them by the sounds that come ringing forth from our buildings that we have something more worth worshipping than football teams or rock groups.

The atmosphere of the father's house which greets the return of the Prodigal Son in Luke 15 is one of festivity and celebration. 'And they began to make merry' (v.24); 'Now his elder son... heard music and dancing' (vv.25, 29).

This is a picture of what the church's worship should be like. We cannot form a basis of teaching on salvation from this story and ignore the father's comments, 'It was fitting to make merry and be glad' (v.32). God clearly endorses singing, dancing and feasting. Not only does he approve of them but he ordained the feast of booths as a statute. 'You shall rejoice before the Lord your God *seven* days' (Lev 23:40–41; also Deut 16:14–15). Moses' first words from the Lord to Pharaoh were, 'Let my people go, that they may hold a feast...in the wilderness' (Ex 5:1; see also Ex 12:14, 17; 23:14).

A football fan may behave in an uninhibited manner as a sign of loyalty to the team he follows, whereas the same person in church, as a follower of Jesus, would hesitate to react in the same way. If, however, he stood in the terraces in the same way as he stands in church, people might well wonder if he was a fervent supporter.

If the church is lacking in joy, then the angels certainly make up for it: 'I tell you, there is joy before the angels of God over one sinner who repents' (Lk 15:10). As unredeemed creatures, they must sometimes scratch their heads when observing how we, the redeemed, fail to be joyful in our privileged position (1 Pet 1:12). Society doesn't help us in this. It actually trains us to be non-responders. We don't have to respond to the TV—we can sit passively in front of it; in school, I was told only to speak when spoken to, for children should be seen and not heard, and in many churches silence is equated with reverence. Yet silence is so rare during the worship in heaven that its one occurrence had to be recorded (Rev 8:1).

The term 'deep joy' is common among Christians in describing a state of mind. When it comes to praising God, our contained joy needs to find expression. If it remains deep it is incomplete. For instance, there is a big difference between thinking thanks and actually expressing it. When someone gives you a present, you wouldn't dream of standing there thinking it was enough that your thought-processes were communicating the words, 'I'm deeply grateful.' In the context of praise, joy is essentially a vocalized expression: 'His praise shall continually be in my mouth' (Ps 34:1). God has put a hole in our mouth to let the fullness out!

An absence of joy and music in Scripture often correlates with a time of spiritual bondage (see Is 16:10; Ezek 26:13). In Revelation 18:22, part of God's judgement on Babylon is that no music ever be heard there again.

In Jesus' time, under Roman domination, the temple worship had become ritualistic and corrupt. In Babylon, worship became redundant as they hung up their instruments and 'sat down and wept' (Ps 137:1–4).

The church has also been held in captivity. The joy and victory in worship, which has been conspicuous by its absence, is returning because people are experiencing these realities as God renews his church. Every revival in Scripture is paralleled with a restoration of music (2 Chron 20—Jehoshaphat; 2 Chron 29–30—Hezekiah; 2 Chron 35:1–19—Josiah; Ezra 3:10–13—Zerubbabel; Neh 12:22–47—Nehemiah; Amos 9:1–13—Amos). Today we are seeing a fulfilling of the prophecy in Amos 9:11 (Acts 15:16) as Davidic principles of worship are being rediscovered and implemented. (For a fuller discussion of the Davidic background to our spiritual worship, see David Fellingham, *Worship Restored* [Kingsway Publications 1987].)

THE WILL

The conflict with feelings

Though worship incorporates various aspects of our being, it should operate from the will. Too many people allow their worship to be governed by how they feel. It is piping hot or tepid, depending on how good or bad they feel. We must learn how to transform our feelings or they will transform us.

Worship must always be set in motion by the will. David says in Psalm 34:1, 'I will bless the Lord at all times; his praise shall continually be in my mouth.' Sometimes, starting to worship can be like starting a car on a cold morning. In may require effort and persistence before the vehicle becomes mobile. Without perseverance, feelings can immobilize us.

The psalmist frequently stirred his soul to praise (Ps 42:5, 11). Occasionally we will have to grab hold of our soul and give it a good shake—rather like a tablecloth full of crumbs. Isaiah 61:3 talks of 'a garment of praise for the spirit of heaviness'. A garment has to be put on, which speaks to us of a deliberate act to counteract negative feelings.

There is always a temptation to allow our feelings to assert themselves. Scripture is not short of people who clearly understood the importance of the will in worship. Jehoshaphat (2 Chron 20:12–22), instead of allowing fear of invasion to consume him, used praise as a weapon to help combat the enemy. Jesus (Mt 26:30), knowing his death was imminent, stirred and strengthened himself with a hymn of praise. Paul and Silas (Acts 16:25–34), after being beaten, late at night and within earshot of possibly unsympathetic listeners, praised God.

Like the priests who carried the Ark on their shoulders, we must shoulder responsibility for doing our part in raising our voices to lift the name of Jesus and not to wait for a more conducive or charged atmosphere before opening up.

The aroma of our worship

In the Tabernacle in the wilderness, we have a vivid picture of worship. The Holy Place was separated from the Most Holy Place by a veil. Each time the priest entered the Holy Place, he was required to sprinkle incense onto the hot coals on the altar of incense. The reaction of the two combining would produce a perfume which passed through the veil into the Most Holy Place (the presence of God).

The cost of our worship

The incense used was very expensive and since the priest had to burn it each time he came into the Holy Place, worship became an expensive process. Scripture gives us examples again of the expense of worship. Abraham was prepared to withhold nothing and to give everything, including his only son (Gen 22:16); David said, 'I will not offer burnt offerings to the Lord my God which cost me nothing' (2 Sam 24:24); David was despised for exhibiting his thanks to God so excessively through dance (1 Chron 15:29); Mary was ridiculed for using a whole jar of ointment, the equivalent of a year's income, to anoint Jesus. This lavish demonstration was merely a token of the value and worth she placed on him (Mk 14:3–9); Jesus was mocked and scorned while carrying out the ultimate act of self-sacrifice and giving (Lk 23:35–37).

The sustenance of our worship

The incense placed on the altar by the priest would not burn if the coals had lost their heat. The coals of our Christian life are Bible study, prayer, fellowship, service, etc. and if they grow cold, the aroma of worship cannot be produced. God requires 'a *perpetual* incense before the Lord' (Ex 30:8). Paul speaks of our worship being maintained daily in Romans 12:11, 'Be aglow with the Spirit.'

THE BODY

Worship—from the inside out

Clapping and dancing can no more produce true worship than kissing and hugging can produce true love. These are results not causes. Yet internal attitudes of worship should produce external expressions, just as a man's love for his wife should be identifiable in terms of verbal appreciation, embracing and giving presents. A man needs to communicate his love for his wife if the relationship is to blossom. Similarly, for worship to be real it must be internal, but if it is to continue to be real, it mustn't remain internal.

In Scripture, the body was used to help express worship. Spiritual attitudes gave rise to physical action:

(a) Standing

Respect (1 Kings 8:22); thanks (1 Chron 23:30); readiness (2 Chron 7:6); steadfastness (Ps 134:1); confidence (Rom 5:2).

(b) Kneeling

Supplication (1 Kings 8:54; Mt 15:25); reverence (Ps 95:6); repentance (Ezra 9:5); prayer (Acts 20:36; 21:5); submission (Is 45:23; Rom 14:11; Phil 2:10); sacrifice (Eph 3:14).

(c) Bowing down

Gratitude (Ex 4:31; 2 Chron 20:18); adoration (Ps 95:6; Mt 2:11); blessing God (Neh 8:6).

(d) Prostration

Homage (Gen 18:2); awe (Lev 9:24); worship (Josh 5:14); repentance (Josh 7:6); supplication (Ps 44:25); confession (1 Cor 14:25).

Note: the three Hebrew words for 'worship' occur 217 times. They are also translated as: stooping, crouching, falling down, beseeching humbly and doing obeisance. The main Greek word for 'worship' occurs fifty-nine times and also involves the idea of bowing down.

(e) Lifting hands

This was done to convey various sentiments: asking and receiving (Ps 28:2; 88:9; Is 1:15; Lam 2:19); surrender (Ezra 9:5; Job 11:13; Lam 3:41); sacrifice (Ex 29:24–28 [here the sacrifice was raised above the head and the whole body was involved in a swaying motion]; Ps 141:2); desiring God (Ps 143:6); new life (Heb 12:12); war (Ex 17:11–13); prayer (1 Kings 8:22, 38, 54; 2 Chron 6:12, 19; 1 Tim 2:8); vowing (Dan 12:7); ministering to God (Neh 8:6; Ps 63:4; Ps 134:2); ministering to people (Lev 9:22; Lk 24:50); divine power (Ex 7:19; 8:5; 9:15, 22, 29; 10:21).

It can also:

(i) Aid concentration. Jesus in Luke 11:2, 'When you pray, *say*...'—not *think*. Words tend not to wander like thoughts do! If speaking our prayers instead of just thinking them can help attentiveness, then the involvement of bodily action(s) to accompany our singing can similarly sharpen concentration.

(ii) Reinforce the words. As well as preventing passivity, an action of

the hands can affirm what is being sung with the lips. For example, encouraging people to either cup or extend their hands in a gesture of receiving while singing *I receive Your love* (SOF no. 226), can help them to realize that receiving is something *we do*. If you ask someone to hand you a book, their efforts to bring it into your possession would be frustrated if you stood there with arms folded. Receiving depends on *you*.

My first encounters with this particular expression of worship caused me to think it would take a crane to get my hands in the air! I was reluctant to develop in worship, rather like the caterpillar, who, on seeing a butterfly swooping overhead, said to himself, 'They won't get me up in one of those things!' It took God only one day to take Israel out of Egypt but forty years to take Egypt out of Israel! Thankfully it didn't take God that long to show me that it was for my own good that I worshipped in mind, *body* and spirit.

(f) Clapping hands

This was a mark of: joy (Is 55:12); wrath (Num 24:10; Ezek 21:14, 17); victory (Ps 47:1; Lam 2:15; Nahum 3:19); warfare (Job 27:23); acclamation (2 Kings 11:12).

This last example was in the setting of a coronation, where the people *applauded* the king. The same kind of non-rhythmic clapping is encouraged in Psalm 47:1, 'Clap your hands, all peoples...' (The Hebrew words are the same in each case, meaning 'applaud'.) There may be times in a meeting when there is a welling up of praise in the congregation, culminating in spontaneous applause to the Lord. At other times you might call for a standing ovation to express appreciation to Christ our King, but such expressions require correct timing, as they should really be the result of an overflow of the heart.

Encourage thoughtful use of clapping. In some churches, a strange duality exists where people sing, 'Clap your hands all you people,' but don't do it.

Check 'careless' clapping. Loud, vigorous, synchronized clapping can be an empty substitute for people giving the affections of their heart to God.

During a time of spiritual warfare, other weapons can be used alongside prayer. As we direct our thoughts against the enemy's activity, praise, clapping, the spoken word of God and dancing can also be used to unfasten evil's hold. As we clap, we can hit out at the enemy's strongholds and pull them down. There can be spiritual repercussions resulting from these physical actions (Ps 18:34; 144:1, 'He trains my hands for war').

(g) Dancing (our responsibility)

Dancing, as a form of worship, should be (i) an outward demonstration of the change God is bringing about in our lives and (ii) a means of giving thanks to him for that change.

Sometimes, cause for concern about the genuineness of this ministry has been expressed, when some of its practitioners have been known to be spiritually immature. In some churches, caution about its use, for fear of it merely becoming a vehicle for exhibitionism, has led to its non-practice or discontinuance. Though we might question the validity of such objections to participating ourselves, it calls for an awareness of our responsibility as we exercise this ministry.

We must also realize that a prerequisite to 'dancing in the spirit' is 'walking in the spirit' (see 1 Jn 1:7) Some have become participants in order to gain a sense of freedom and victory, instead of their dancing being an expression of the freedom and victory they are *already experiencing* in their daily lives. An understanding of the biblical background to dance might help to bring us into a more meaningful expression of it.

In Scripture, dancing is a sign of: victory (Ex 15:20; 1 Sam 30:16); joy (1 Sam 18:6; Ps 29:6; Eccles 3:4; Lk 1:44; 6:23); celebration (2 Sam 6:5, 14, 16; 1 Chron 15:29; Ps 42:4); gratitude (Ps 30:11; 114:4); praise (Ps 149:3; 150:4); love (Song 2:8; 6:13); new life (Is 35:6; Lk 1:41); merry-making (Jer 31:4, 13). Its prolonged absence was a sign of spiritual decay and apostasy (Jer 48:33; Lam 5:15).

(i) Dancing and celebration: There were two attempts to carry the Ark of the covenant into Jerusalem. The first time, it was carried irreverently and carelessly—on a cart—and God's wrath was incurred (2 Sam 6:6–7). God's anger was not kindled, as some people have thought, by the dancing and merrymaking but by the slovenly attitude of those who held his presence with them so lightly.

When on the second occasion the Ark was borne with the reverence due to Almighty God—on the shoulders of the priests—there was nothing to prevent God from accepting it, and delighting in the festivity and in David who 'danced before the Lord with all his might' (2 Sam 6:14). It is interesting to note that before he danced, he took off his royal outer garments and set them to one side. There has to be a setting aside of any pride or preconceptions before such self-abandonment to God is possible.

Unless the whole congregation is taught how to enter in to dance, it can become the practice of a special few. There is no correlation between an inability to dance and lack of spirituality. Most people just don't know what to do. One tip to at least get people mobile is to encourage them to move from one leg to another in time to the music.

(ii) Dancing and prophecy: David's dancing was prophetic. Normally in a royal procession the king would ride at the front, while a dancing clown heralded his coming. It was unthinkable that the king should take up any other place, and outrageous that he should take the place of the clown, since a clown is an object of wit and ridicule and has no status.

David's dance was a visual foretelling of how Christ the King was going to come as a servant and be treated with contempt. 'Michal...saw King David leaping and dancing before the Lord; and she despised him in her heart' (2 Sam 6:16). Someone may be giving himself in an unrestrained manner to God in worship while onlookers project their reserve and become critical, seeing only the externals (Jesus' entry into Jerusalem [Lk 19:38–40]; Jesus' anointing [Mk 14:4–5]; Jesus' death [Mk 15:29–32]).

Having crossed the Red Sea, Moses is given fresh insight into the character of God (Ex 15:1–18). He expresses this in a prophetic song. This word is then extended in the form of a dance by Miriam and the women (v.20). The prophetic utterance is unpacked even further and finally stated in another song (v.21).

Similarly, there are various ways in which we can reply to God's word. For example, a passage of Scripture may be sung, followed by a response from the musicians playing prophetic music and lastly interpreted by dance and movement. There needs to be a more exploratory approach to how we can flow with what the Spirit may say.

(iii) Dancing and spiritual warfare: In Scripture, the feet were often depicted as a weapon of war: 'Through thy name we tread down our assailants' (Ps 44:5); 'It is he who will tread down our foes' (Ps 60:12); '...and the serpent you will trample under foot' (Ps 91:13); 'I have given you authority to tread upon...all the power of the enemy' (Lk 10:19); 'Yield...your members to God as instruments [weapons] of righteousness' (Rom 6:13); 'The God of peace will soon crush Satan under your feet' (Rom 16:20). (Also 2 Sam 22:37, 39; Ps 47:3; Is 10:6; 14:25; 26:6; Micah 1:3; Col 2:15; Heb 2:8.)

What we do with our hands and feet in worship can have impact in the heavenly realm. Physical actions in the visible world can have spiritual consequences in the invisible world.

THE VOICE

Singing

In Scripture there are over 120 references to singing.

Unity

A combination of singing the same words and tune at the same tempo can, in a moment, create a sense of oneness. As we sing, we are not trying to bring about unity but express and realize the unity we already have. Singing is an act of articulating the condition of our relationship. If there is disharmony, this is what God hears. Two musical instruments need only be slightly out of tune with each other for a dissonance to result. This is as discomforting and irritating to our ears as it is to God's when listening to the discord in relationships being expressed in worship. Paul tells the early Christians to live in harmony with one another first and then 'together you may with one voice glorify the God and Father of our Lord Jesus Christ' (Rom 15:6).

Power

Generals throughout history have been known to stir their troops to sing as a means of both raising morale and of striking fear into the enemy camp (1 Sam 4:5). When invasion looked likely, Jehoshaphat did exactly this. He 'appointed men to sing to the Lord... as they went out at the head of the army' (2 Chron 20:21, NIV).

Faith

Sometimes our singing can depend on external circumstances such as a big congregation being present, our favourite songs being chosen, the musicians playing well, or being in a good mood. The only requirement for singing is a voice—and not necessarily an in-tune one: 'Make a joyful *noise* to the rock of our salvation' (Ps 95:1–2).

A true worshipper worships God unconditionally. The Israelites in Babylon made certain stipulations before they could sing. 'How can we sing the Lord's song in a foreign land?' (Ps 137:4). As a result, worship was in a state of collapse: 'We hung up our lyres' (v.2). They had resigned themselves to it; so much so, that even the torments of their captors could not incite them to sing (v.3). Sometimes, we can feel so oppressed that we are unable to take up the invitation of the leader to sing. We can end up conceding to the torments of the enemy. If Satan is trying to make us captives, by bombarding us with negative thoughts, Jesus would urge us to fight back. He always has our highest good in mind when he bids us to do something which goes against the grain. As we begin to sing, we may feel so dry that the words seem to stick in our throats, but singing can be a valid means of willing ourselves out of darkness into light; from unbelief into faith.

Integrity

Without the reality of God in our hearts there can be no reality in our singing. We may sing with great zeal, but if we attempt to honour God with our lips while our hearts are far from him (Mt 15:8), he warns us, 'Take away from me the noise of your songs' (Amos 5:23). When the Israelites worshipped the golden calf, Joshua mistook the fervent singing to be the sound of war (Ex 32:18–19).

Sensitivity

Just as enthusiastic singing must not necessarily be regarded as an indication of spiritual life, so a reluctance to sing cannot be looked upon as a sign of spiritual lukewarmness. For example, someone may be grieving over the death of a friend. When leading, we must learn how to be sensitive to people's predicaments. We must not ignore them, regarding their presence as an embarrassment, but provide opportunity to identify with them and 'weep with those who weep' (Rom 12:15).

New Testament references to singing

The last supper (Mt 26:30; Mk 14:26); Paul and Silas (Acts 16:25); 'I will sing with the mind...' (1 Cor 14:15); 'Each one has a hymn...' (1 Cor 14:26; 'Sing psalms and hymns and spiritual songs' (Col 3:16; Eph 5:19 [psalms were songs from the Old Testament Psalms. Hymns were songs expressing New Covenant truth, and spiritual songs were spontaneous prophetic songs or singing in tongues]); Jesus singing praises to his Father (Heb 2:12); 'Is any cheerful? Let him praise' (Jas 5:13); the new song (Rev 5:9–10; 14:3); song of Moses (Rev 15:3); song of heaven (Rev 19:1); Jesus and his early followers praised God with Old Testament Psalms (Lk 20:42–43; Acts 1:20; 13:33, 35; Rom 15:9).

Loud voice

This act usually denoted: faith/victory (2 Chron 20:19); sadness (Ezra 3:12); joy (Ezek 3:12; Ps 81:1; 84:4); repentance (Neh 9:4); righteousness (Ps 33:3); thanks and praise (Lk 17:15; 19:37); authority (Acts 14:10); veneration (Acts 14:11); proclamation (Rev 1:10); worship (Rev 7:10) and supplication (Rev 6:10).

Shouting

This was a shout of faith (Josh 6:16, 20—the walls of Jericho); triumph (1 Sam 4:5—a weapon to strike fear into the enemy camp); praise (Ezra 3:11—the people began their time of praise with a loud shout); joy (Ps 32:11; 47:1; 71:23; Zeph 3:14; Zech 9:9).

In times of spiritual warfare, the shouts of faith and triumph can pull down spiritual walls and advance God's kingdom. Leaders must be ready to lead the people with festal and victory shouts. For example, *'Christ has died! Christ is risen! Christ will come again!'* or *'Your kingdom come! Your will be done on earth as it is in heaven!'* Don't be afraid to cause the congregation to repeat these if at first they are only done half-heartedly.

In intercession, the weapon of shouting can be like the nails in the devil's coffin after our prayers have laid him to rest.

Laughter

'Then our mouth was filled with laughter, and our tongue with shouts of joy' (Ps 126:2).

Singing in tongues (languages)

The term 'singing in the Spirit' given to one form of singing can be misleading as it suggests that other forms are not 'in the Spirit'. Being 'in the Spirit' is not something we *do* in a *meeting* but something we *are* in our *lives*. Those who sing in this way for the first time must never become so preoccupied with the question: 'Was I really singing in the Spirit?' that they fail to ask, 'Am I really living in the Spirit?' In the same way, no one can ask whether or not they've got the Holy Spirit without being prepared to determine whether the Holy Spirit has got them!

For a more detailed study of this form of singing, see page 118.

Prophetic singing

A practical outline of this form can be found on page 115.

The new song

This term is synonymous with the terms 'prophetic singing' and 'the song of the Lord'. Its occurrence in Scripture meant that the singer(s) spontaneously uttered words and music which were either sung solo or accompanied by other instruments (Ps 33:3; 40:3; 96:1; 98:1; 144:9; Is 42:10; Rev 5:9; 14:3).

INSTRUMENTS

This is a list of the main biblical references to instruments in worship. It is not comprehensive.

Ex 15:20; Ps 33:2; 57:8; 71:22; 81:2, 3; 92:3; 98:5–6; 137:2; 144:9; 147:7; 149:3; 150:3–5; Rev 5:8.

A balanced line-up

Avoid having an over-abundance of one type of instrument (e.g. five guitars, one violin, three trumpets and one piano).

Learning related instruments

One of the guitarists could learn to play the bass or electric guitar; a clarinettist the saxaphone; a pianist the synthesizer; an oboist the English horn.

Buying new instruments

If one player has an ability to play another instrument, but doesn't own or have access to one, look into the possibility of purchasing one with church funds to add colour to the music. If extra percussion was made available (chinese bells, bongos, bell-tree, glockenspiel, chime-bars, etc.) one of the singers could play them.

Miking up

If there is a shortage of microphones, use them on the softer-sounding instruments (violin, clarinet, etc.). These can often get drowned by the other instruments, particularly drums. If you can't hear the other instruments well, you're likely to be playing too loud. Drop the volume of your playing, unless the others are playing too timidly.

Togetherness

If there is more than one guitar, similar strumming patterns must be played—*either* on-beat or off-beat accents. Often songs don't 'take off' because the musicians are not agreed on how the song should be treated rythmically.

**Example 1: When the Spirit of the Lord is within my heart* (SOF no.604).

On-beat	Em		B^7
>	> > > >	> > > >	>
When the	Spirit of the Lord is with-	in my heart, I will	sing....
Off-beat			
>	> > > >	> > > >	>
When the	Spirit of the Lord is with-	in my heart, I will	sing...

**All numbered examples are to be found on the cassette accompanying this book.*

An inexperienced guitarist, rather than trying to follow the strumming of other more skilful guitarists in a roughshod, pressurized way, might be best just playing the accents of the strumming patterns.

Fit in with the style of the song

Pianists don't always have to play the melody, especially if (a) there are enough vocalists to carry it, and (b) the song requires 'chunky' rythmic playing. Just stick to the chords rather than trying to grapple with the melody as well.

Sensitivity

All the instruments don't need to be played all the time. This particularly applies to the kind of lead-line player such as the woodwind, brass, strings or synthesizer player who insists on playing the melody only (and on every verse). Play brief, thoughtful phrases intermingled with a few bars of silence. If an instrument drops in and out, it is more likely to be heard than when it is there all the time:

(a) Using the technique of 'answering phrases'.

Example 2: River wash over me (SOF no. 468).

(b) Playing in the chorus sections and last verse only. This prevents the song from peaking too early. If the most important climax of the song comes in the fourth verse, it's no good everyone playing loudly in the second verse. To contribute effectively to the shape of a song, you might have to discipline yourself to playing only in certain sections. Refrain from following the crowd, and use your initiative.

Make full use of the various elements of music to give greater expression

Explore the full range of the instruments' dynamics (see pp. 115–116).

Tying up loose ends

Begin and end songs neatly. Don't creep in cautiously or melt away like a jelly. In order that both congregation and musicians can hear the leader's instructions between verses, the lead instruments (flute, oboe, etc.) should not play and the guitarist(s) and pianist should refrain from playing any distracting melodies.

Don't forget to worship

Your playing should be an extension of your praising. This isn't easy since you are concentrating on the leader, the music and your instrument. Musically underscore the significance of the words. Explore the full range of dynamics to do this.

Playing isn't necessarily the most important part of the meeting

Enter into the rest of the service. Don't switch off when you're not directly involved. God might want to speak to you specifically, so don't hide behind your role as musician.

Conclusion

In praising the Lord with the mind, heart, will, body, voice and instruments, God wants our worship to be multi-faceted, fully-orbed, many-sided and richly-coloured.

5

Raising People's Expectancy

What might God do?

Before leading a time of worship, ask people to discuss with those around them (in groups of two to four, perhaps) what they think God might do in the meeting. Get each group to come up with about five ideas, and then maybe write these responses on an overhead projector acetate and discuss them, adding brief, helpful, encouraging comments.

God changes lives

Unless worship changes us, it isn't worship.

Transformation

We become like whatever we worship. If it is money—greedy; if sex—lustful; if the home or the car—proud; if yourself—selfish; if Jesus—Christ-like. As we worship Jesus we are promised that 'we all . . . beholding the glory of the Lord, are being changed into his likeness from one degree of glory to another' (2 Cor 3:18). Here, the word 'glory' conveys the idea of the weight of God's presence being pressed into us—transforming us—like an object being pressed into plasticine and leaving an imprint. God is holy (whole and complete). True worship should cause us to take on his likeness. Because God is powerful, worship releases power in us. God wants his attributes to be made manifest in us.

Conviction

In Isaiah 6:1–8, Isaiah is engulfed by God's presence. He becomes aware that he is 'a man of unclean lips' (v.5). When we have a confrontation with the divine, sin which we have tolerated, or hurts which we have buried in our subconscious, can rise to the surface.

Purification

Our first reaction can be to erase or further suppress such thoughts, but it is healthier to allow them to be revealed. As we hold ourselves under God's loving searchlight, there may be things in our past which we dare not face because we will have to relive the pain associated with them. Deep forgiveness and cleansing only come when we allow God to flush away all the spiritual debris in our minds.

God doesn't leave Isaiah in a pool of hopeless, introspective self-examination, but pronounces him forgiven (v.7).

Vision

Isaiah's response is to offer himself to God for a life of mission. God purified him *for a purpose* (v.8). Unless we become motivated to tell others about Christ, worship is in danger of becoming a therapy session during which we receive spiritual massage to gain a sense of well-being. The church exists for the benefit of non-members too, and unless worship stirs us to evangelism, we will become trapped in a ghetto of celebrations.

Reconciliation

Worship should embrace honesty. In Matthew 5:23–24, Jesus says that if we know someone has something against us, *we* must attempt to rectify the grievance before we even start to worship. God regards external piety and internal hypocrisy as a repugnant mixture. Our worship is supposed to be like a sweet-smelling perfume in God's nostrils, not a stench.

The morning after having led a brief time of worship in one meeting, I received a phone call to say that a married couple, who had been at the service with their children, were so touched during the singing of *Jesus, Your love has melted my heart* that they called their solicitor to stop their divorce proceedings going ahead.

Liberation

Praise can draw us out of ourselves. It can help us to move from darkness into light. Praise is the dark room where our negatives can be turned to positives.

Not only can praise silence our own negative attitudes but those of others also. Once, a friend of mine was standing in a shop queue. Some of the people in the queue were complaining about the prices of the various items they were about to purchase. When it was his turn to be served, the shop assistant told him that there was 10p off one of the items he was buying. He casually said, 'Oh, praise the Lord!' at which point all the grumbling ceased, to be replaced with looks of astonishment.

Psalm 8:2 says, 'From the lips...you have ordained praise because of your enemies, to silence the foe and the avenger' (NIV). The effectiveness of our warfare depends on the degree to which our lips have been used as a launch pad for God's weapons or the devil's—to speak the language of praise or the language of criticism. This is why we are urged to 'continually offer up a sacrifice of praise... the fruit of lips that acknowledge his name' (Heb 13:15). The quality of our lives determines whether our praises will be like water-cannons or water-pistols in the face of the enemy.

God changes situations (praise warfare)

Behind the world scene are powers and personalities. God wants the weapon of praise to be successful and effective in preventing the forces of evil from advancing.

> Let the high praises of God be in their throats and two-edged swords in their hands, to wreak vengeance on the nations and chastisement on the peoples, to bind their kings with chains and their nobles with fetters of iron, to execute on them the judgment written! (Ps 149:6–9).

God wants our praises to achieve something!

About nine years ago, I was involved with a mission in a Sussex village. One afternoon the team were praying about a group of lads who were disrupting the evening meetings by noisily congregating in the toilets. As we prayed, we felt we should go (male and female) and pray in the focal point of unrest—the boys' toilets. Praying there proved unpleasant because the place smelt as if it hadn't been cleaned out for months, but as we prayed, we also sung songs of Christ's victory over Satan, and after about fifteen minutes, we sensed a kind of breakthrough and decided to leave. Much to our amazement, we all realized that the smell had gone! Later, we discovered that there was a lot of occult activity in the village and possibly this area of the building had become occupied by evil spirits inciting the disturbances each night, preventing the gospel from being heard. (Many believe that occasionally evil spirits manifest themselves in the form of displeasing odours.)

God led us to use the weapon of high praise 'to silence the foe and the avenger' (Ps 8:2). God inhabits the praises of his people and when the toilet became intoxicated with his presence, the enemy could not remain. After that night, many of the youngsters, including the ring-leader of the gang, became Christians.

In 1 Samuel 7:7–11, 2 Chronicles 20:2–23 and Daniel 6:6–28 we also see God's people being attacked. In each case, praise is a key factor to the enemy being routed and destroyed. In spiritual battles we need to use spiritual weapons, not carnal weapons. At times, usually when we fail to recognize the spiritual nature of the conflict, it will be very tempting to employ the wrong kind of ammunition.

An example of this is the fellowship which gathered together to pray about a pornography shop which had opened in their community. It must have been tempting to rush in with verbal guns blazing, demanding that the proprietor close down. Instead, they recognized that the battle was the Lord's (2 Chron 20:15) and so they got together to do spiritual warfare, praying and praising for a few hours. The next day, they were astounded to hear that during the night the shop had burnt down! God had carried out a modern-day Sodom and Gomorrah and had responded to their high praises 'to wreak vengeance' and 'to execute the judgment written'. The results of this fellowship's praises don't sound dissimilar to those of Paul and Silas' midnight praise-party in jail during which the foundations shook (Acts 16:25–26), and also the great shout of victory prior to the walls of Jericho collapsing (Josh 6:20).

Another example of this 'battle in the heavenlies' occurred when I was leading an inter-denominational celebration. The following weekend, there was to be an 'occult fair' for 700 people in the town. During the celebration, we raised our voices to God in high praise, asking him to stop this forthcoming event. It was tremendous to see some of the local newspaper headlines during the next few days: 'Occult Fair cancelled at Twelfth Hour', 'Hotel closes Doors on Occult Festival.' Not only did the establishment which was to host the event withdraw its support, but so did a second venue, engaged at the last moment!

God is re-educating his church about the weapon of high praise in these days. It travels faster than light, goes anywhere in the world, always hits its target, often has a delayed detonating mechanism and is completely invincible. Yet there are conditions to its success. For praise warfare to make any indentation on the enemy's strongholds, what matters is *righteousness* (right living)—not volume! Also, *we* must not try to gain a spiritual breakthrough. Instead, we must with faith declare Christ's victory already won for us at Calvary. We must not try to gain ground which Christ has already given us. 'He disarmed the principalities and powers... triumphing over them' (Col 2:15). Let's not get tricked by the devil into fighting a war which is already won.

God makes himself known (worship and evangelism)

The church commissioned in worship

'And when they saw him [Jesus] they worshipped him... And Jesus came and said to them, "... Go therefore and make disciples of all nations..."' (Mt 28:17–19).

The church birthed in worship

'We hear them telling in our own tongues the mighty works of God' (Acts 2:11). Here the disciples are extolling and praising God. Their words are not addressed to men. Set against this background is Peter's sermon and the conversion of 3,000 people.

The church directed in worship

> While they were worshipping the Lord and fasting, the Holy Spirit said, 'Set apart for me Barnabas and Saul for the work to which I have called them.'... So, being sent out by the Holy Spirit... they proclaimed the word of God in the synagogues of the Jews (Acts 13:2–5).

The church given revelation in worship

In 1 Corinthians 14:24, Paul is looking at the use of spiritual gifts in worship. He is saying that when God's people begin to worship as they ought—being led by the Holy Spirit into receiving and exercising God's gifts—then the unbeliever will see supernatural reality at work. 'He will worship God and declare that God is really among you' (v.25).

This demonstration of God's power through us is provisory though. Without love, spiritual gifts are like beautiful decorations on a tatty Christmas tree. '*If* we love one another, God abides in us' (1 Jn 4:12). The unbeliever is very sensitive to how much people in a fellowship are indwelt by the love of Christ. It is often this unconscious influence of Christ in us which wins people to God. A few of my friends have become Christians during 'the peace' at an Anglican service. Some might think this a strange moment to make a confession of faith, but they all said that it was at this moment—when people were expressing the love of Christ to one another—when they realized Jesus wasn't in an ancient tomb but alive in his body.

The church empowered in worship

In Acts 16:25–34, there is another example of people being converted during worship. Paul and Silas, despite the uncomfortable surrounds of a prison cell, were singing God's praise when they were involved in a divinely-initiated jail-break. As a result of God's power shaking the foundations of the prison, the jailor and his family came to Christ. When people see us praising God as we ought, they will come to us and echo the jailor's remarks, 'What must I do to be saved?' Jesus promised it would be so. 'When I am lifted up... [I] will draw all men to myself' (Jn 12:32).

After a visit to one church, I received a letter which further underlined for me the connection between worship and evangelism.

> Towards the end of last Sunday evening's service, our minister had a feeling that there was someone outside the church in whom the Lord wanted to work. So, he took us out onto the steps of the church facing the High Street and led us in a time of worship with his accordion. (This is something we have never done before!) As we sang, one person stopped and listened, then came up the steps and joined us. We are praying for his salvation.

In one sense this surprised me, but in the light of Scripture it didn't. 'He put a new song in my mouth, a song of praise to our God. Many will see and fear, and put their trust in the Lord' (Ps 40:3). It may not only be out onto the steps of the church that the Lord wants to lead us but into the market place and streets of our communities, to retrieve ground and lives which the enemy has taken.

God makes his plans known

Let's imagine that a being from outer-space, on visiting planet Earth, comes across a guitar. Unless our inter-galactic friend knows what a guitar is and how it should be treated, he might think it is a means of transportation and sit on it. In order for us to get a response from something, we must treat it *according to its nature*. Maybe at times God isn't responding to us in our worship because we don't treat him properly.

Just as there is a code of conduct to be observed when meeting the Queen, so there is a correct procedure for approaching the King of kings: 'Come into his presence with *singing*' (Ps 100:2). 'Enter his gates with *thanksgiving* and his courts with *praise*' (v.4). These are not optional extras but vital necessities as we begin to move into God's presence.

We won't hear from God or sense his presence unless we come with a heart of praise. Being in a negative frame of mind can desensitize our spiritual perception. We can be in God's presence and not be aware of it. This was the case with the disciples on the Emmaus road. At first they were down-hearted, but as they began to open up and converse with Jesus 'their eyes were opened and they recognized him' (Lk 24:31) and 'he was known to them in the breaking of the bread' (v.35). In John 21, the disciples are despondent after an unsuccessful night's fishing. Verse 4 reads, '...Jesus stood on the beach; yet the disciples did not know that it was Jesus.'

Praise reveals Jesus. He is found in the praises of his people (Ps 22:3). As we praise him, he becomes clearer and his voice more discernible.

God often speaks in the context of worship:

(a) As Joshua worshipped the Lord, it was revealed to him how to take Jericho (Josh 5:13–14; 6:2–5).

(b) After music ministered to Elisha, he was able to move in the prophetic, resulting in Jehoshaphat receiving direction from God (2 Kings 3:11–17).

(c) 'I will incline my ear to a proverb; I will solve my riddle to the music of the lyre' (Ps 49:4). This underlines the relationship between music and prophecy. Therefore, musicians need God's anointing just as much as preachers.

(d) In a worshipful environment, God makes it clear that Barnabas and Paul are to be sent on an evangelistic campaign (Acts 13:1–3).

During the worship at one Saturday night meeting, a lady stood up and asked everyone to pray for her minister who was finding the resistance to change in her home church soul-destroying. As we prayed, we moved into praise warfare. One of the phrases used in the time which followed, as we engaged in evicting any entrenched enemy activity from her church, was, 'The windows of the church will be opened up.' The next morning, she phoned her minister to see how that morning's service had gone. He told her that the night before, when he'd been preparing his sermon (it turned out that this had been at the same time we'd been interceding for him), he'd felt a strange urge to cross out the talk he'd been preparing and to start another headed, 'The windows of the church will be opened up!' Worship can prepare us for divine insight.

God breaks spiritual bondage

In the hands of God music can break spiritual bondage.

Two friends of mine, Colin and Joan Veysey, told me the story of when they were staying at a couple's house. One evening, the couple went to minister to a converted gypsy, leaving Colin and Joan in the house. While they were out, other gypsies who were angry about the conversion put a curse on the house. Throughout the evening, Colin and Joan felt increasingly oppressed, though they didn't know why.

At one point, Colin went to the bathroom. While he was away, Joan was knocked to the ground and held there by an invisible force. Meanwhile, Colin was sensing that God was telling him to sing *In the name of Jesus*. When he returned to find Joan on the floor looking as white as a sheet, he quickly realized they were involved in spiritual warfare and began to sing. Slowly, as they both sang about Christ's defeating Satan, the heavy atmosphere lifted.

It is interesting to note in this incident, that God directed Colin to *praise* and not to *pray*. At times, the warfare will become so intense that the *guns* of prayer need to be backed up with *tanks* of praise (see Psalm 8:2).

In 1 Samuel 16:14–23, Saul is being troubled by an evil spirit. Whenever it came near him, he became downcast. His only relief from these attacks was when David played some music. It wasn't because of the standard of David's playing that the spirit left, but because of the quality of his life. This was why there was such a powerful anointing on the music and it was this that the evil spirit recognized.

After one meeting, a lady told me that a year ago, her husband and son had been killed in a car accident. Since then, she'd been consumed by an overwhelming sense of grief. Though she had mourned the loss of her family, the grief had now become a gripping influence in her life. She went on to say that the first time she'd felt released from these sorrowful feelings was during the worship that evening.

Westernized Christianity trains us to operate mainly from the mind. We are rightly encouraged to think things through logically. Music, though, has little to do with the powers of reason. It reaches us at a deeper level of our being. Each of us probably has a favourite piece of music which moves us deeply. In the area of spiritual bondage, music has an important role to play at that deeper level of human existence, in being a practical tool in God's hands to free us.

God breaks physical bondage

When Jonah was swallowed by the whale, his last words of prayer before being vomited on to dry land were, 'But I with the voice of *thanksgiving* will sacrifice to thee...deliverance belongs to the Lord' (Jon 2:9). Thanksgiving opens up the way for God to bring us deliverance.

I was once involved in an interdenominational meeting in Lancashire. During a time of thanksgiving and praise to God, I encouraged people to greet each other. One gentleman came up to me and told me he'd just been healed. He had irons on his legs but he'd left his sticks by his seat.

At a similar meeting in Ulverston, during the worship, someone felt that God wanted to heal a person's back problem. Afterwards, as a group of us were praying together and thanking God for the evening, one person interrupted the prayer with a gasp. The Lord had healed them and we weren't even praying for them! Psalm 50:23 says, 'He who sacrifices thank-offerings honours me, and he prepares the way so that I may show him the salvation of God' (NIV).

God's presence and glory come down

In 2 Chronicles 5:13–14, the glory of God came upon the worshippers in the form of a cloud. A friend from Africa told me that something similar once happened at his church. The glory of God appeared in a cloud and a holy fear gripped everyone as they looked upon the sight. I'm not advocating that we encourage people to seek such appearances in our meetings, but we should be expecting God to manifest himself among us.

I'm sure the coming of God in such a tangible way in 2 Chronicles was not too divorced from the instrumental and vocal praises. God is omnipresent. That is, he is in the building where we meet for worship just as much as when we are not there, but from our human angle, there are times when God seems more tangible. Why is this?

As we meet for worship, most of us will be unaware that radio waves are passing through the building. Tuning in to those radio waves requires the use of a receiver. God is like those radio waves and he has provided music as a receiver to help us sense his presence and his voice to tune us out and to tune him in.

The very first notes in 2 Chronicles saw God's presence come down. Sometimes we can feel that we need to create an atmosphere to get God here. For some, the very act of raising hands can be a sign of trying to pull God's presence down. We need to see that God initiates true worship in us. Jesus told us that the Father *seeks* worshippers (Jn 4:23). So this takes all the strain out of our efforts. In fact, Jesus said he would never leave us. We are his tabernacle—his dwelling place. We need to learn how to *relate to his presence*. Psalm 22:3 tells us that God is enthroned on the praises of his people. As we unite in heart and voice, it is as if our praise becomes the throne on which he resides.

God increases faith

In commanding us to worship him God is not ego-centred. He has our highest good in mind. As we sing a song such as *Jesus, we enthrone You*, it is for our good that we see him where he is—on the throne, in charge of our lives. He is wanting to speak to us through such songs to say, 'That's right, my child, I have the keys to life and death. Your future is in my hands.'

As we declare things about God, it can strengthen us. As we come in faith, with truth and by the Spirit, we can change. It isn't so much that *he* needs to hear us proclaiming the facts of his protection and provision, but that *we* need to hear and believe what we're singing so that our burdens can go. For instance, as we sing about God being a fortress and a deliverer in the song *Praise the name of Jesus,* then it should affect the way we view the mortgage, rising prices, imminent redundancy and coping with the kids. We need to let the words speak to our hearts so that after singing these truths we have a fresh sense of God being with us and for us. When we sing a song such as *The steadfast love of the Lord*, we must declare it as truth, as if it was God himself saying to us, 'That's right my children, so you can trust me in this difficult situation, can't you?'

There is a big difference between simply singing a few songs and actually worshipping. God wants our faith to be built up. That's why Ephesians 5:18–19 instructs us to sing to one another. It's a way of releasing faith in each other's lives. The fruit of it will be increasing faith, making us stronger in God.

In Genesis 15:4–5, God told Abraham that he was to have many children, but his faith must have dwindled when he considered the physical condition of his ageing wife. Romans 4:20 says that as he gave praise and glory to God, his faith increased. That is, his ability to agree with what God said grew. The mountainous problem of his wife's barren womb became a molehill *as he praised God*.

Giving priority to praise

Praise reduces doubts and produces faith. It can give us a more godly perspective on seemingly gigantic problems. We see this as David faced Goliath. David's preparation for this encounter began a long time before. The confidence which enabled a mere youth like David to address Goliath with such impressive rhetoric (1 Sam 17:26) did not emerge overnight. He had committed himself to praising God from an early age: 'I will ever sing praise to your name and fulfil my vows day after day' (Ps 61:8, NIV).

It was this discipline of praise which grafted power into his very being, enabling him to deal with the evil spirit which troubled Saul (1 Sam 16:23). Later, startling success on the battlefield was the result of continuous praise in his life. His words of faith, 'This day the Lord will deliver you into my hand' (1 Sam 17:46), flowed from a reservoir of praise. What he lacked in physical stature and years he made up for in spiritual power and faith. All too often our faith wavers because it isn't issuing from a *consistent* life of praise. The more consistent our praise, the more deadly our warfare will be. So let's 'bless him all day long' (Ps 72:15, NIV).

6

Worship Flows out of Relationships

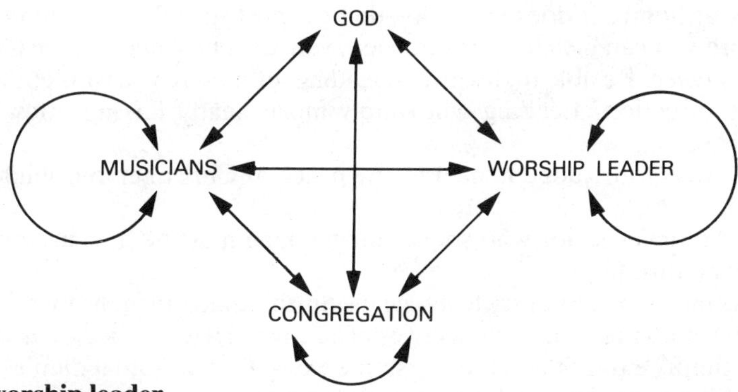

The worship leader

To lead effectively, you must be secure in your relationship towards:

1. Yourself

* Have a healthy self-acceptance. You can't have for others what you haven't got for yourself.

* Personal confidence is essential. This comes from an inner conviction of God's calling which sustains us through difficult times. (Overconfidence is as bad as a lack of confidence.)

* Don't be apologetic for your ministry.

* Don't project self-doubts. Don't read into situations things which don't exist. The sighting of a stony face in a congregation can easily be taken personally, when actually the person might simply have a headache. (Doubt your doubts and believe your beliefs!)

* Don't respond to any 'negative static' you might be picking up. Don't get drawn into vindicating yourself. Leave that to God.

* Don't be over-defensive about your ministry.

2. God

His love: You can't bring others further than you've been yourself. You can't persuade others of the love of God if you don't know it yourself. Be a source of refreshment for the thirsty.

His forgiveness: Unless you have appreciated what God has done for you, you might use your position to elevate yourself. Jesus said that he who has been forgiven much, loves much. We have *all* been forgiven much.

His holiness: Arguably, God's most important attribute is his holiness. In Revelation, the heavenly hosts don't cry, 'Love...is the Lord,' but, '*Holy*...is the Lord.'

*Your ministry cannot be separated from your lifestyle. It should be lifelong and consistent; not one hour long. 'If your Christianity doesn't work at home, it doesn't work—don't export it!' (Howard Hendricks). Before you can be a man before men, you must be a man before God.

His voice: Be able to discern his leading, otherwise you won't be able to bring direction. Leading will simply mean neatly linking a few songs together.

* Trust your judgement. Let the peace of Christ be your guide (Col 3:15).

* An ambassador who speaks for the king must be in constant touch with the throne.

His ministry: Don't try to gauge the Spirit's ministry in the meeting. He always does more than we see. Especially when we are tired or unwell we may think, 'I didn't feel the worship went well, therefore it didn't.'

* Don't give up on those who on the surface never appear to budge. We are called to be obedient, not necessarily successful.

* Minister by faith, not by sight. The church may be going through hard times.

* Don't jump to conclusions. The worship may have been 'flat' because of tiredness, not sin.

3. The minister

* In allowing you to lead the worship, the minister is placing trust in you. Don't misuse it by doing anything which you know might cause him problems. Remember, the buck stops with him!

* Don't announce that you're going to move in a particular direction and then openly ask permission of the minister. You might find that the carpet is pulled from beneath your feet. Clear it *beforehand* whether or not you can encourage dancing, singing in tongues, etc. Agree on the general direction beforehand, too.

* The tail shouldn't wag the dog! (Sometimes the tail isn't connected to the dog.) Don't speak harshly to the people. Leave any admonishing to the minister. You are there to comfort the afflicted, not to afflict the comfortable.

* Don't over-run the time allotted to you unless you are permitted to do so.

* Have comeback after the meeting. There may be limitations in evaluating what God did, but we can assess what we did. Let's not settle for second best. Let's eliminate anything which is hindering the people from giving their best.

4. The musicians

* The leader must be someone who understands the talents and temperaments of those in his care. He must know their capabilities and limitations; how to stretch them without breaking them; how to bring out the best in them. He should be able to discern when they are losing confidence and enjoyment.

* His aim must be to further the spiritual and musical development of those in his care. To fulfil this task he must first:

(a) have laid down his own aspirations. Jesus '*emptied* himself' (Phil 2:7).

(b) have been given authority over those in his charge. (Ability and anointing without delegated authority leads to frustration.)

(c) have been accepted by those under him.

* The leader must build up a good rapport with the group. Though Jesus was called 'Master', he called them his friends.

* Don't correct them within earshot of the congregation. Don't make negative comments immediately after the meeting. Discuss these at a later date when they are less tired and therefore more receptive.

* The leader's discipline of the group must be firm but caring.

5. The people

* Gain their trust. Your ability to lead depends on their willingness to follow.

* Trust God in them. If people's faces appear to be as motionless as sunbathers', don't go on first impressions. Lead them gently. Don't pressurize them. Let the music do the work.

* Don't try to impress. Be a God-pleaser not a people-pleaser.

* Don't be continually watching how the reluctant minority are reacting. Don't let the devil build up caricatures of them. Everyone is needy, even those 'difficult' people. It would revolutionize our relationships if we related to everyone as if they were lonely and insecure.

* Know and accept their limitations. You can't draw out worship which isn't there. You can't lead non-worshippers into worship. The question is: 'Do they want to worship?'

* Don't go at the rate of the slowest. If you do, you won't go anywhere because they're likely to have their heels dug in!

* Encourage individuals who pray, exercise a spiritual gift, or give a testimony, to speak up. Where appropriate, repeat a paraphrased version of it if you sense that many couldn't hear.

* Quickly rectify any relationship you've damaged. Keep lines of communication open. Build bridges with anyone who doesn't see eye to eye with you. Pray that they'll ask the right questions.

The music team

1. Organization

The head musician: Under David, 4,000 musicians in twenty-four divisions were involved in praising God (1 Chron 23:5–6). Leaders were appointed to oversee them (1 Chron 15:16, 22; 16:5; Neh 12:42). Often we have problems with organizing just four musicians, let alone 4,000, because there are too many chiefs and not enough Indians. One chief musician must be appointed.

The musicians: They were selected (1 Chron 15:16; 16:41; 2 Chron 29:25; Neh 7:1). Not just *anyone* could play or 'have a go'. It was a serious undertaking. Some churches emphasize this with the laying on of hands (1 Tim 4:14). The musicians are in effect set apart for service, as in 1 Chronicles 25:1.

The main requirement should always be calling, not talent. The qualities one should look for are sanctification, submission, sensitivity and skill. The priorities are: (a) character (spiritual) and (b) ability (musical) —in that order.

2. Commitment

The musicians': The Old Testament musicians were loyal and faithful in their duties (1 Chron 6:32; Neh 12:45). Their dependability didn't fluctuate. Today, church musicians shouldn't be allowed to drift in and out of the music group, playing when they feel like it. Leaders mustn't be kept wondering whether certain musicians will turn up at the last minute or not. Those who don't attend the rehearsal shouldn't expect to play in the meeting.

It was the musicians' place to minister *continually* before the ark (1 Chron 16:37). This song of praise to the Lord never ceased. We must remain resolute even when we are tired or our enthusiasm is flagging. In Nehemiah 10:39 they made a resolution not to neglect their post. There will be the temptation to allow our attendance to drop off when the going gets tough, the services monotonous and the people unresponsive. Stick-ability is tested in the lions' den! It's not how you start that matters, it's how you finish. We should encourage each other constantly to withhold nothing (1 Chron 13:8).

The church's: The levitical musicians and singers were supported from the people's tithes (Ezra 7:16; Neh 11:23). They were spiritually provided for with wine and oil (Neh 13:5) and materially looked after with homes (Num 35:1–8). Similarly, church leadership should show concern for the music department: (a) spiritually—encouraging the encouragers, and (b) practically—ensuring that bad equipment is replaced if it is frustrating them.

3. Fellowship

The depth of commitment which the Old Testament musicians had when we read of them joining together in Nehemiah 10:28–29, cannot develop if we meet only to practise. In some churches, the music team meet as a house group. This is in addition to rehearsals. Of course, this means that the other house groups lack skilled musicians, but it does enable them to grow as a unit praying for one another, reading the word and worshipping together.

If we want to minister *life*, we need to become what we want the people to become—united. When people dwell in unity, there the Lord commands the blessing (Ps 133:1, 3). What we minister will be as rich as our relationship, and a relationship is as good as its communication.

4. Ministry

In Exodus 3:14 God refers to himself as 'I am', not 'I do'. Doing comes out of being. We minister what we 'are' in our relationships. Harmony or disharmony will be reflected musically. You cannot hide it. The effectiveness of our ministry will be proportionate to how much each musician has been able to:

Work for the good of the others: Obstinacy or a desire for recognition can minimize and blunt our ministry. 'Unless a grain of wheat falls into the earth and dies, it remains alone' (Jn 12:24).

Open up to the others: Most people don't admit their weaknesses. Some musicians feel they would—if they had any! We all have good emotional defences (often arising from hurts) which can stop us receiving and expressing love. The caring atmosphere of the group can help to dismantle them lovingly.

Receive correction from others: Relationships are the means by which God shapes us for better things. God can't help 'strong' people. He can use the team environment as a pressure-cooker to bring the truth about ourselves (good and bad) to the surface. It may have to be pointed out to us that patience, which we think we seldom lose is continually being mislaid! We may not realize we've always been looking for credit. None is more unaware of pride than the carrier.

Appreciate the others: Musicians often under-estimate the extent to which God has gifted them.

When these principles are working in us, they will energize our ministry. Music, without these elements, might still produce a response from the people, but it will not be life-changing.

5. Teamwork

Building a team requires us to:

Be

v**U**lnerable

commun**I**cative

Loyal

involve**D**

appreciat**I**ve

accepti**N**g

Growing

pr**A**yerful

hones**T**

r**E**spected

Available

hu**M**orous

6. Service

'There are few Christians who can carry a full cup with a steady hand' (Bishop C. T. Ryle).

Some believe that Satan was responsible for the worship in heaven. He wasn't happy serving and stirred up the other angels. We may not be disruptive, but if we have a desire to be rewarded or a continuous need for reassurance, then we are not servants and are unfit to minister. Servants try to make *others* successful (Heb 6:10). Beautiful music played by a proud musician is like jewels on an ugly hag.

We can ascertain whether or not we are truly serving by the lack or presence of inadequacy and vulnerability we experience when, for example, there are too many guitarists so we have been asked to sing instead; or when we are the most proficient player—until a newcomer turns up.

The more a musician hides behind a role to cover up spiritual needs, the worse the needs become. The more he clings on to his instrument, the less God will be able to use him.

The musicians of the Old Testament didn't serve only with their music. They helped out in other areas (1 Chron 9:28–33; 25:8; 26:29). Some of them were gatekeepers, which entailed watching over sheep (1 Chron 9:26–27). Similarly we, after the meeting, should keep a watchful eye open for anyone who needs counselling. They also dealt with the people's tithes (1 Chron 9:26). Are we trustworthy?

7. Training

Before and after the age of twenty-five when the levitical musicians began their service (Num 8:24), they received musical instruction (1 Chron 15:22; 25:6). The result was that they were 'skilful' (1 Chron 25:7). Psalm 33:3 enjoins us to 'play skilfully'.

In no department of life do we receive all our knowledge at once. It is gradually accumulated and revised. Musical talent needs nurturing. Just as apple trees don't produce apples all year round, so church musicians should not be continually expected to bring freshness to the worship without periodical in-service training to keep them sharp and to broaden their horizons. This is especially so of those who feel they don't need it! If we are not teachable, we run the risk of spiritual fatigue.

There are courses available from time to time designed to envision, enthuse and equip those involved in worship (Eph 4:12). These are advertised in the Christian press.

8. Holiness

There should be no daylight between what we say and what we are. God wants his word formed in us so that if we're knocked, the word comes out. If we want our music to be anointed with power, we can't afford to sin. God will not allow an unholy person to carry his holy presence (1 Chron 15:2, 14). Before the Levites could qualify to carry the ark, they had to take an oath to remain holy (Neh 10:29). They wore fine linen robes to symbolize the nature of this oath (1 Chron 15:27) and cut themselves off from any sources of spiritual contamination (Neh 10:28), just as we are called to put off the old nature and put on the new (Col 3:9–20).

The congregation

In Exodus 33:15–16, Moses says to God, 'If your *Presence* does not go with us... what else will distinguish me and your people from all the other people on the face of the earth?'(NIV). The *presence of God* is to be the distinguishing mark of God's people. We are to be his dwelling place. Something deep in the heart of the outsider recognizes the unconscious warmth and influence of God's presence among Christians in a meeting. (They also sense his absence!)

This presence is conditional: '*If* we love one another, God abides in us'

(1 Jn 4:12). How can God show love to us if we don't show love to others? It can't be done—the circuit is incomplete.

Lukewarm relationships

Worship and relationships belong together. Worship should be securely undergirded with love. As we come together our worship should have the features of Christ about it—a body where each member feels connected. There is no such thing as a *single* Christian. As a Christian, to be is to be related.

We are also a family and therefore our worship should have a homely feel about it. Very often, though, the independence and individualism of society infiltrates our meetings. We are reserved and undemonstrative. Unless we begin to express the love which Christ has put in us, it will become impotent. We can sing, 'Let there be love shared among us,' but this can keep the reality at arm's length. What might be more fitting is to encourage people to go to one other person in the meeting and tell them one thing about them which they appreciate (without any compliment having to be returned). Communicating love almost amplifies that love. Though worship is loving God in the presence of others, it is also loving others in the presence of God.

Unforgiveness

The leader of a house group went to his minister to request the removal of a lady who had become a negative influence on the group since stating her dislike for the group's expressive worship. The leader was astonished to find that the minister regarded the leader's unforgiveness as the root problem. Reluctantly he asked God to forgive him. Soon afterwards, the leader attended a conference where, during the first session of worship, he was distracted by someone behind him whose singing and clapping seemed to be rather excessive. He turned round to see the lady from his group!

Forgiveness opens doors and takes down barriers, but unforgiveness creates barriers. Worship must never become a substitute for obedience to God. Love must remain the over-riding condition of true worship. 'To obey is better than sacrifice [worship]' (1 Sam 15:22–23). The context of Ephesians 5:19 (NIV), 'Sing and make music in your heart to the Lord,' is that we 'submit to one another' (v.21). Similarly, 'Sing psalms, hymns and spiritual songs' (Col 3:16, NIV), is preceded by verses 13–15 which command us: 'Bear with each other and forgive whatever grievances you may have against one another. Forgive as the Lord forgave you.' God wants our worship to be living and our living to be worship.

Part Two

Preparation for A Meeting

7
Prayer

On your own—away from the meeting

Jesus' *public life of power* was in direct relation to his *private life of prayer*. His *power before the people* was in many respects the result of his *prayer before his Father*. The disciples' request, 'Lord, teach us how to pray,' may have been partly born out of seeing this connection. They didn't ask how to heal or perform miracles. This was one of those rare insights for which the disciples are not renowned. Sometimes our eyes can be drawn to the 'flowers' of someone's ministry without first seeing the roots from which they spring. When God is working *through* someone, it is because he is working *in* them. Therefore, just like Jesus, we need to spend time on our own during the week, worshipping our Father. As we continually maintain the freshness and glow of the Spirit, our leading of worship will have a new cutting edge. ('Be aglow with the Spirit'—Rom 12:11.)

With the musicians—before the meeting

Blessings in worship come from:

(a) Prayer
(b) Putting God first
(c) Wanting the highest good for the people
(d) Planning and practice

No blessings in worship come from:

(a) Little prayer
(b) Wanting to be thought highly of
(c) Being touchy with each other
(d) Poor preparation

David knew this responsibility for preparation. In 1 Chronicles 15:1 we read, 'He prepared a place for the ark [presence] of God.' We too must prepare our lives for his presence before we can lead.

Prayer is often the one ingredient of preparation which tends to get rationed. Since Satan used to be involved in the worship in heaven, he knows the potential authority and power to those who will worship. He will attempt to stop the church from worshipping God and very often hits out at those responsible for leading worship. In 1 Samuel 18:10, David was playing an instrument, and we are told in 16:23 that the music protected Saul against an evil spirit. In 18:11, the evil spirit causes Saul to throw a spear at David. Yes, leading worship can put us in a very vulnerable position! Therefore, we need to prepare ourselves in prayer.

Pray for yourself

For cleansing

In 2 Chronicles 5:11; 29:15 and Nehemiah 12:30, those involved in leading worship purified themselves. In 1 John 1:9 we are told to *confess* our sins. We must do this immediately rather than thinking that God may be more approachable when the guilt resulting from our sin is wearing off. The blood of Christ is the only substance in the universe which can cleanse sin (1 Jn 1:7). It is the Christian's bar of soap.

For freedom

(To serve, not to impress.) If you are feeling tense before leading worship, you are likely to transmit that sense of inhibition to the people. *You've* got to be what you want them to be. In order to bring others to a point of surrender before God, you must be yielded.

For expectation

'You do not have, because you do not ask' (Jas 4:2). If we expect nothing to happen, God is likely to prove us right!

In order to raise the people's expectation for what God wants to do in the meeting, you must first experience your own faith being stimulated. You can't bring them further than where you are.

For power

Ephesians 6:10 says, 'Be strong in the Lord.' In our preparation for meetings, the temptation is to feel that we must have highly-developed skills of communication, a varied repertoire of songs and arrangements and carefully-planned services. Just as we can't fight germ warfare with a gun, or atom bombs with a fly-swat, so we can't fight Satan's power with *our* methods. Yes, we do need to develop skills, but God very often uses our weaknesses, not our strengths. Satan is not vulnerable to our methods, but he is to the weapons which God has made available for us to use.

The weapons of our warfare (2 Cor 10:4)

* Use the name of Jesus: 'You come to me with... a spear... but I come to you in the name of the Lord (1 Sam 17:45). David rejected Saul's offer of armour for God's. We don't tag the name of Jesus onto the end of a prayer to give it credibility and to guarantee it being heard in heaven. We first ensure that our petition is worthy of the name of Jesus.

* Use the blood of Jesus: 'They have conquered him [Satan] by the blood of the Lamb' (Rev 12:11). Satan is not in hell. He is in the heavenly places. As we enter into this evil realm with prayer and worship, enemy forces can attempt to join in and disrupt, like insects attracted to a light bulb. The blood of Christ keeps them off us.

* Use the authority of Jesus: 'Behold, I have given you authority to tread upon serpents and scorpions, and over all the power of the enemy' (Lk 10:19). We should not be asking *Jesus* to bind the enemy. If we are in Christ *we* have his authority. Michael Harper in his book *Spiritual Warfare* (Kingsway Publications) parallels the woolly thinking on spiritual authority to a tennis match in which God and you are playing tennis against Satan. Suddenly, Satan strikes the ball down the middle of the court, between God and you. God shouts to you, 'Yours!' When it comes to binding the enemy, the ball is in *your* court. God says, 'Over to you.'

* Use tongues: 'For we do not know how to pray as we ought, but the Spirit himself intercedes for us' (Rom 8:26). We simply just *do not know* how to pray. Our mind wanders, we have mixed motives, half our mind is analysing what the other half is praying wondering, 'Do you really mean that?' We are wondering what others are thinking of our prayer. Many Christians would admit that their prayer life is not all it could be. Isn't it lovely that God wants to meet us at the point of one of our deepest needs—knowing how to pray? Prayer in tongues is pure and effective prayer because it is the Holy Spirit communicating with the Father and Jesus, without the restrictions of our mind. Through the act of speaking, *we* offer up the prayer.

* Use praise: 'The Levites... stood up to praise the Lord, the God of Israel, with a very loud voice' (2 Chron 20:3–19). Following the news that various armies were about to destroy them, Jehoshaphat called Judah to fast and pray (v.3). Out of this time of prayer came a prophecy declaring God's faithfulness, to which the Levites responded with loud praises.

Men of war have always known the power of song to revive and invigorate them when morale is low. Praise is the Christian's secret weapon. It can link our impotence to God's omnipotence. When we are like coals which have lost their heat, singing can help to fan the flames of enthusiasm again, enabling us to take the glow out to the people and into our private lives.

As we come to the end of a theme in prayer, a few songs of praise can draw strands of thought together, capsulizing and cementing them.

* Use spiritual gifts: 'The secrets of his heart are disclosed' (1 Cor 14:24–25). The gifts of the Holy Spirit are a means of God exposing the works of Satan, as well as building up the church. For instance, one word of knowledge can reveal adultery while another can pinpoint a need for physical healing.

Pray for the people

'Fight the good fight' (1 Tim 6:12).

Many Christians are quick to see the need for prayer before outreach events, but slow to apply the same principle to their weekly corporate worship. Our meetings are often far more public than the human eye can tell. Unless the devil is dealt with (Mt 4:10; Jas 4:7), he is free to roam among us, injecting the atmosphere with apathy and heaviness. He is keenly interested in what we are doing in our corporate acts of worship. When a group of people are touched by God's power in worship, he has got trouble on his hands. Is it no wonder, then, that we will sometimes sense resistance, feeling that we just can't worship, or that as we do, we're gripped by strange feelings of annoyance, unworthiness or tiredness? The devil is always punctual. Let's see that he doesn't get in!

If our prayer before a meeting is merely a kind of ritualistic rubber-stamp, then we shouldn't be too surprised if we're not experiencing the kind of release God wants us to have. Our prayers need to be like fire-extinguishers, not water-pistols, asking God to drench the atmosphere of the building with his Spirit, so that people begin to feel refreshed even as they sit there before the meeting starts.

The victory needs to be won *beforehand*. It's too late doing battle *during* the meeting.

(*Note*: Deal with the enemy *briefly*. Remember, we go to a meeting to focus our thoughts on God and therefore the less attention we give the devil the better.)

Intercede and take authority on the people's behalf. Seek their welfare. Don't taint your prayers with your own insecurities: 'I hope I do OK. I hope people like the songs I've chosen.' Some people may arrive at the meeting, having just had a conversation which wasn't at all edifying, possibly having said something about someone which was neither helpful nor necessary. Some may have just finished watching a film which they could well have done without watching. As you pray, clear away the 'sludge' on their behalf, or at least pray that at the beginning of their time with God, they will clear away any rubble preventing God from building new things in their lives.

Pray for the building

'Sanctify yourselves and the house of the Lord' (2 Chron 29:5).

We need to pray for the places where we meet as well as for the people who meet there. In Acts 2:2 the Holy Spirit filled *the house* where the early Christians were meeting. This is equally true of Satan's power. Having gained entry, he can induce an atmosphere of disquiet and heaviness. We must, however, be careful not to attribute every drab atmosphere to the devil. Discernment is necessary. Yet we must be open to the need for prayer in buildings where maybe for generations there has been *the worship of worship*, where the aesthetics of the music and outward forms of ritual have taken precedence over the One worshipped. In such cases, it may be advisable to pray in the pews, choir stalls and organ loft. Satan is not always easily noticeable when entrenched. Learn to *identify the enemy* and deal with him swiftly and boldly.

Pray for direction and inspiration

The son of a great violinist himself became a great violinist. His father had never taught him and when asked why, his father sadly replied, 'He never asked me.' If God knows about the service, we ought to find out what he thinks first (Eph 5:17; Col 3:15).

Preparation for leading worship should take just as long as preparation for preaching. The worship leader, like the preacher, should be able to come sensing the general direction the Lord wants us to take. God doesn't want us to come with everything preconceived. Don't try to put the Spirit in a strait-jacket. Remember, it's *God's* meeting.

During a time of prayerful listening to God prior to the meeting, particular areas of need and ministry might be revealed. It's as if in our times of celebration, a cake is being baked and sometimes God will let us in on some of the secrets of the recipe beforehand. It very much depends on our alertness to such promptings of the Holy Spirit as to whether we recognize those ingredients or not. We can easily miss or dismiss them as being the result of our minds doing overtime. Many of God's treasures are being lost or trodden underfoot because we are not accustomed to the many ways he might communicate with us. These various elements may be:

Words of knowledge: Divine information about people's physical, emotional and spiritual condition.

Words of direction: Aims which the Lord wants us to accomplish in the meeting.

Allegorical visions/pictures: A message from God in the form of symbolic mental impressions or outlines. (The meaning of these will very often come from the person sharing the details of the 'picture'.)

The beginning of a new song: Maybe a few lines which the Lord adds to throughout the meeting. The finished version may come at an appropriate point in the meeting, as the person launches out in faith, joining these words to a melody which is sung unrehearsed.

Other gifts of the Holy Spirit: As we pray for people to be used, we should be prepared to be the answer to our own prayers.

Note: These 'words' need to be *offered* for testing and not presented 'thus saith the Lord'! The leadership must agree on whether it will be right to share those things in the meeting or not. Whether we are expecting the Lord to forewarn us in such ways and are able to pinpoint them when he does, is very much a case of 'be it according to your faith' (Mt 9:29).

With the musicians and leaders—before the meeting

In a church I used to attend, after the musicians have had their final rehearsal, they meet for a further twenty-five minutes with everyone else involved in leading the meeting: the vicar, curate, preacher, organist, reader of the lesson and the person leading prayers.

Apart from having a unifying effect, it helps everyone to realize that there is no insignificant part of the meeting. (Even the notices can be done with an anointing. If they are not, they are usually read in a boring manner.)

One house group each week is responsible for welcoming people at the door, handing out prayer information sheets and hymn books, as well as collecting them afterwards. Meanwhile, other members of that house group will join the prayer meeting asking God to protect and empower every aspect of the meeting.

Prayer is like a tug-of-war, so there is strength in numbers. Jesus' promise, 'Wherever two or three are gathered . . .' cannot be claimed if we are on our own. Worship is an arena of activity. We are in the frontline, but behind the scenes the devil and his accomplices are agonizing away, trying to render our efforts ineffective. There's also a great cloud of witnesses urging us on while angels are being released to fight. We fail to come sufficiently prepared at our peril!

The congregation's preparation

The rest of the fellowship should be continually encouraged to come similarly prepared. This would help to combat the 'spectator mentality' so common in many churches. Some people expect a service to run like a well-oiled machine and when things are not going smoothly, they slip into the back-seat driver syndrome, becoming agitated and critical, without realizing they have not given a moment's thought in prayer before the service. We can easily become part of the problem instead of part of the answer.

How corporate is the worship in your fellowship? Outside one church, the noticeboard once read:

Ministers—the congregation
Assistants—Rev. Smith and Rev. Jones

Does this reflect a biblical understanding of your church, its ministers and ministries? (See Eph 4:11–16; 1 Cor 12:4–7, 12–26.)

So often, our meetings can be like a bus. The minister is in the driving seat, the congregation sit like passengers, looking at the backs of each other's heads, and the ticket collector comes round for the offering. Essentially, we leave it all to *the* minister. Instead of a 'body' ministry, we end up with a 'big ear' ministry; instead of an alive organism, a tired individual.

Someone once wrote:

The rector is late. He's forgotten the date,
So what will the faithful do now, poor things?
They'll sit in a pew with nothing to do
And sing a selection of hymns, poor things.

Following these guidelines, our worship can be as deep corporately as it is individually. Just as the Magi came bearing gifts in worship, we should come prepared to give (Mt 2:11).

8

Planning

1. Preparation for any meeting begins at home. The it'll-be-all-right-on the-night attitude can be a licence for laziness. In some circles, leading

off-the-cuff is regarded as a sign of spirituality. Though we shouldn't shun the ability to do things instinctively, let it be noted that organization (administration) is a spiritual gift (1 Cor 12:28).

2. Begin by stripping the format down to its bare bones.

* Are there aspects of our meetings which hinder us from becoming tuned in to God's presence? We often pray, 'Lord, give us our daily bread.' Daily bread means *fresh bread daily*, not *stale crumbs*. We should periodically review and assess whether the diet we are feeding the people is nourishing or not.

* Do we always serve up the same atmosphere for people to come in and go out to? There's more than one possibility: quiet songs of worship, boisterous songs of praise, quiet receptiveness to God, piano, organ or group playing/singing (The music at the end of the meeting should be a response to the atmosphere at that moment. It may be right not to have any music at all.)

* Is there a theme for the meeting which everybody involved in leading is clear about?

* Is there any padding which could be omitted? Might three hymns be too many, especially if they contain archaic language which is likely to alienate any unchurched newcomers?

* Does everything have significance? For instance, what is the purpose of each song? Do they link to the theme? (Do they have to?)

* Do the readings relate to other aspects of the meeting—a solo song, a sketch, a testimony?

* Is the offering or the reading of God's word always in the same place? It isn't good enough to say, 'But we've always had it there.' When the format becomes predictable, we are in danger of becoming familiar with holy things.

* Does the talk *always* precede the worship (or vice versa)?

* Are prayers always led in a similar way? If one person has traditionally led them, maybe occasionally a group could lead them. You could also ask the congregation to split into groups to pray, sharing their own needs first, before turning their thoughts to social issues further afield.

* Are there any unwritten laws which are inhibiting us? For instance, do we sing choruses sitting down and hymns standing up? Are choruses led from the front while hymns are not? (In some churches, when a group leads choruses, the minister sits down and lets them get on with it. Some might think that the minister physically detaching himself from the group is a sign that his blessing is not fully with this style of worship. Encourage the leaders to stand with the musicians.)

* Do we only sing songs through twice (and three times if revival

comes!) or do we *always* sing songs through more than a few times? We can get into a rut either way. Someone once asked a friend of mine why he led songs repetitively, and his tongue-in-cheek reply was that we need to get used to singing this way because in heaven 'day and night they never cease to sing, "Holy, holy, holy is the Lord God Almighty"' (Rev 4:8).

* There may be a reason as to why we do things in a certain way *now*, but we have to be aware that we can slowly become like a needle on a record player, caught between the grooves of ingrained tradition.

3. Be flexible. Cultivate a more spontaneous approach. Have various options up your sleeve (see *Song Lists* under the next heading).

4. Anticipate how to handle certain situations.

The inappropriate. For example, you are in the middle of a time of adoration when a prayer for someone's bad back seems to take the meeting off onto a tangent. (It may be right to pray for this problem, but not just then. The Holy Spirit often has a direction which he wants us to follow and fit in with. It is up to the leader to help those who are less sensitive.) In such an event, people's attention might be refocused on the previous unfinished theme with an appropriate song, a prayer, or a few words. If you have been side-tracked, don't draw attention to those responsible as you may put them off contributing on another occasion. It is better that people *do* contribute, even at the risk of being off-beam.

The unexpected. (This doesn't mean the second coming!) Know how to operate and lead people in the gifts of the Spirit. At one inter-denominational celebration, a message in tongues was given, and the worship leader froze. He came from a fellowship where such gifts weren't openly practised. Instead of saying something along the lines of, 'As in New Testament times, let's wait for God to give us the meaning of this message,' he panicked and announced the number of a song. (Avoid the formula, 'When in doubt—sing a chorus.') At this point, one of the leaders stepped forward and calmly said, 'We've had a message from the Lord and we need to wait for the interpretation.' This problem could have been avoided if due preparation had been made.

The mechanical. Know how to deal with worship which is merely going through the motions. Never use pressure tactics to draw worship out of people. If you admonish people for singing without thought, they might respond with more volume but not necessarily worship from the heart. Instead, briefly say something about thoughtful worship *without* reference to their passivity. This will enable them to respond without feeling they're being evaluated. In the privileged position of leadership, we should be affirming and encouraging, not exercising a ministry of rebuke!

If you sense that the words of a hymn are washing over the people without them getting wet, don't be negative about their efforts. You could emphasize the need for a greater concentration and deeper consideration of the words by saying, 'Let's sing those last two verses again. . . .' Read out one or both verses.

5. Think ahead. Announce where possible what is going to happen next. For instance: 'Before we sit for the reading of God's word, let's sing number twenty-three. . . .' This also acts as a signal to the reader to be ready.

6. In situations where some people regard new songs and forms of worship with suspicion, we need to over-prepare so that no ammunition for criticism is handed to them on a plate.

7. Some worship leaders who are musicians just think of the musical side of the worship. Though music in worship is as fitting as laughter in a comedy, it isn't the be-all-and-end-all of the meeting. Be aware of what is happening to people's feelings.

8. As we plan, God's purposes and objectives will become evident.

The tools of the trade

Songs

(a) Don't use songs which you are unsure of or dislike.

(b) Try to become comfortable with different types of songs. Some leaders cause the worship to be predictable because of their preference for one style of music. For example, non-rhythmic or up-tempo. You are not there to play your favourites.

(c) Songs should be chosen carefully so that there are no abrupt changes in tempo or theme. Don't alternate between fast and slow songs or between thanksgiving, warfare and adoration. Use songs to express your worship, not to get people going or calm them down.

(d) Generally, start with a longish song—one with verses and a chorus, like *Rejoice!* (SOF no. 461). This can help people to get going.

(e) You don't have to sing *all* the songs you've rehearsed. One song can be the 'kingpin' of a meeting. The Lord might want you to dwell on a particular song, singing it repeatedly, until people have come into the realization of its message. This may mean that in the time left, you will not be able to play the other songs you've prepared. Letting the Lord minister is far more important than completing your list.

(f) Teach new songs *at the beginning* of the meeting, not *during* the worship. It's hard to both *learn* and *worship* at the same time.

(g) Don't teach by sectionalizing, unless there is difficulty with a melodic phrase. Play the song through once as the people listen. Then get them to stand and sing it until it seems established. Don't be scared of too many repeats.

(h) Know what God is emphasizing in your fellowship at the present time and teach songs which reinforce that.

Song lists

(a) Keep a folder of your notes and music.

(b) Keep an up-to-date master list of songs in alphabetic order. Anyone assisting in leading (vicar, pastor, etc.) should have this list in front of them, so that they don't ask the musicians to play something outside their repertoire.

(c) Group songs in themes and tempos. These can act as pools of songs in which to fish, so that at a glance, you can continue in that particular stream of worship without page-flicking or head-scratching. Some possible themes could be: call to worship, thanksgiving, praise, exaltation, celebration, adoration, seeking and thirsting for God, repentance, forgiveness, healing, commitment, unity and spiritual warfare. It may also help you to indicate with a colour-code which songs are fast, medium-tempo or slow. (There is a helpful index of themes and tempos in SOF Book 3.)

(d) To help the musicians to prepare, give them a copy of the songs you're likely to use. Here is an example of the layout you might use for a particular meeting:

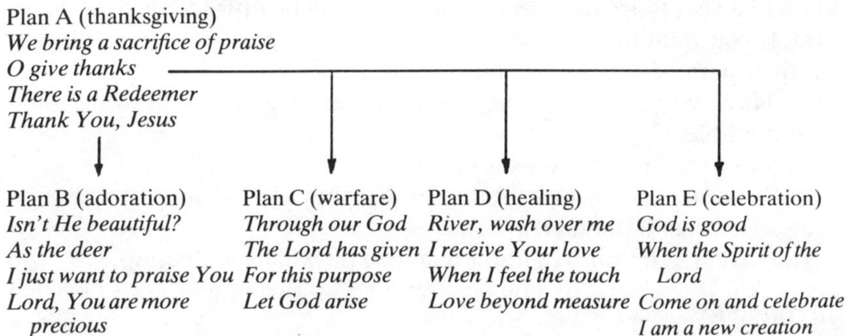

Guidelines: Don't feel that you have to use all the songs in Plan A, or in that order. It may be right after *There is a Redeemer* to continue with Plan D. After a few songs in that section, you may feel that the Holy Spirit wants to minister on the Fatherhood of God. If the musicians are familiar with a song which is not on the list, but which would be helpful at this point (e.g. *Father God, I wonder*, don't feel you can't use it. From here, it may seem right to go into Plan E to sing *God is good*.

Songbooks

(a) Know the number of each song.

(b) Announce it clearly beforehand, or as the introduction begins.

(c) Check the verses. You might find yourself starting a fourth verse which the congregation don't have in their books (numbers of verses do sometimes vary between publications).

(d) Check the words. The version you know may differ slightly from that found in the congregation's songbooks.

Overhead projector

(a) Have someone who knows how to operate it—preferably the same person each time.

(b) Do they know where the on/off switch is and when to use it? Some OHP motors are quite noisy. This isn't noticeable while people are singing, but it can become distracting during a time of silence, or while gifts of the Holy Spirit are being shared.

(c) Check that the words are in focus before the meeting. Can they be read from the back?

(d) Make the operator aware that when people are standing, the verses at the bottom of the acetate may not be visible and will have to be moved up with care.

(e) Work on the basis of 'one song per acetate' whenever possible. When two sheets are used, the changeover can be distracting.

(f) If you want to repeat one of the choruses, announce the number so that the operator can quickly locate it.

(g) Have you got all the acetates for the songs you'll be using (and other possibles)?

(h) Give the operator a list of the songs.

(i) Place the acetates on a table so that they can be quickly identified and transferred to the OHP.

(j) Have a spare bulb ready should one blow during worship.

Microphone

(a) Position your mouth about three inches above and three inches away from it. (When you speak or sing, the air comes out mainly vertically not horizontally.) This position will enable you to be seen as well as heard.

(b) Don't blow or poke it suddenly to check if it's operative.

(c) Don't handle it when talking. This is often a sign of nerves.

(d) Know how to adjust the height of the stand should others who are smaller or taller than you be using it after you.

PA

(a) Who is in charge of mixing the sound for the forthcoming meeting? If different people are responsible for it, a rota should be organized so that you are not always having to check that they are going to turn up.

(b) Leads should be 'screened'. Cheap leads might pick up taxi/police intercoms. In one meeting, just as the leader concluded a time of corporate prayer, a voice came booming over the PA system, 'Message received, over-and-out!'

(c) If you can't hear yourself sing/play, you're likely to focus on this rather than on the job of leading sensitively.

(d) The musicians should be able to play quietly and still be heard at the back. (Many guitarists have to strum all the time because fingerpicking would be lost.)

Fold-back speakers

(a) In some church buildings, because of the position of the PA speakers, the congregation can hear the musicians but the musicians can't hear themselves well enough. If the speakers cannot be repositioned, it might be possible to purchase a few fold-back speakers which can be placed on the ground, facing in the direction of the musicians, so that they can clearly hear each other.

(b) If you are setting the tempo of songs with a guitar or piano, the musicians (especially the drummer) must be able to hear your accents, deliberate changes in tempo and vocal directions.

Your Bible

(a) If the congregation uses one particular version, use the same one. Corporate readings of Scripture aloud can be very effective. (Don't be afraid to get people to repeat the verse or passage.)

(b) Keep one Bible with themes related to praise and worship underlined. Worship occurs 220 times, praise is mentioned 332 and music over 800 times. Worship is the central theme of the Bible.

Your instrument

(a) Buy a stand. It will protect your instrument from being accidentally knocked and damaged. (It will probably cost £10-15.)

(b) Check the tuning. It may have gone out of tune during the pre-meeting rehearsal.

(c) Have you got spare plectrums and strings ready? What about extra capos, reeds, mutes, sticks, etc?

(d) An excellent though expensive capo (especially for twelve-string guitars, to prevent strings buzzing) is the SHUB capo.

(e) If you don't want to be restricted to a microphone on your guitar, have either a Dean Markley Pro. Mag Pick-up fitted (approx. £45) or a C-Ducer for about the same price.

9

Practice

Readiness

Poor preparation consists of either:

(a) Practising without leaving enough time for praying;
(b) Praying without leaving enough time for practising.

In 2 Chronicles 5:11–14, the glory of the Lord filled the temple. Prior to this divine visitation, there was an atmosphere of readiness among the leaders and musicians. The priests had sanctified themselves and those responsible for the music were similarly prepared. The Lord moved among them in a visible and tangible way. If we want to see the Lord manifesting his presence in our worship, we must do all we can to come spiritually and musically prepared. God will not let such readiness go unrewarded.

Group rehearsals

1. When to rehearse

* It is advisable to meet more than once before playing in the weekly service (a) mid-week; (b) a few hours before (for an evening service).

* Between these two rehearsals, each individual should take a little time each evening (even ten minutes would see an improvement) to polish up any rough edges such as difficult chord progressions.

* Each person should attend regularly.

* Stress punctuality. Start on time. Those who are habitually late often

lack vision for the worship.

* The person in overall charge (vicar, pastor, elder, etc.) must meet with the worship leader prior to the practice to discuss the worship. This will help to clarify the direction of the practice.

2. What to rehearse

(a) Mid-week. The main emphasis will be 'nitty-gritty' details such as:

Songs: The majority of songs should be chosen by the leader beforehand so that time isn't wasted in upholding democracy during the practice.

Music books: Make sure there are enough of the same publication for each musician. If one person has *Mission England* and another has *Songs of Fellowship*, the chords may not be the same for a particular song. Sort that out beforehand.

Keys: Some books put certain songs in difficult vocal registers. Prepare the transposed chords before the rehearsal.

Chords: Some versions of songs could be greatly improved with the addition of a few colourful chords. Don't change any chords, however, if it results in the less skilful players feeling out of their depth.

Arrangements: As ideas emerge in discussion, don't attempt to memorize them. Each person should be making a written note of any special details, such as playing one verse softer. In the next rehearsal, time will be saved by not having to repeat such instructions.

Tempos: Songs shouldn't be taken so fast that the congregation can't get their mouths around the words. They shouldn't drag either.

Time signatures: Clarify any likely confusion. Some songs work with either of two time signatures (for example, *Jesus, how lovely You are* can be played in either 3/4 or 4/4.

Words: Both leader and singers need to sing the same words. Some songs can be sung slightly differently (for example, *We have come into this place/house*).

Introductions: Avoid count-ins. One instrument, preferably the piano or guitar, should play either a four- or eight-bar introduction which clearly establishes the right tempo (see *Introductions* p.81).

Solos: Which instrument(s) will play the melody, if the leader instructs the musicians to play an instrumental verse in the meeting?

Which instruments: Don't assume that certain songs always have to be played by the same instruments. A song normally played by the music group could be played on the organ. The group might also attempt to incorporate some hymns into their repertoire.

Hymns: Some hymns have alternative tunes. Double check that you've got the correct version. Hymns can be led in the same way as choruses—by one person or a group. Each verse can be treated differently, as the leader directs.

Modulation (changing key): Learn how to do things in different keys.

Improvisation: More experimentation is necessary in rehearsals. A group of musicians are unlikely to play spontaneously and creatively together in a meeting if they are not doing so in their practice sessions.

In the context of worship, spontaneity is not necessarily spiritual. For example, if you have never played the chord of Em7♭5, then the Holy Spirit is unlikely to suddenly contort your fingers into the required position. Most musicians' ability to improvise effortlessly is the result of years of studying and familiarizing themselves with which scales and modes can be played over certain chords. Some jazz musicians seem to have minds like a library's intricate card-index filing system, but such ability has been gradually developed. We don't have to systemize our approach to playing in such an open-ended way before we make an attempt to improvise. We just need to begin with the level of ability we have. In rehearsals, use some of the chord sequences on pages 128–130 to play to. This will prepare you for such things as singing in tongues.

(b) Just before the meeting. The main emphasis will be on worshipping with the practised material.

The mid-week rehearsal will be a fairly clinical time of dissecting songs, putting passages under the microscope and interrupting songs to make suggestions. This second rehearsal is a kind of dummy-run where we mainly *worship*, having as good a time (if not better) than in the main meeting. Songs should be repeated to allow room for creativity and should flow into each other or into improvised playing suitable for accompanying singing in tongues.

3. How to rehearse

Setting up equipment: Any amplification and equipment additional to the church PA (for example, electric keyboards, bass guitar amps, drums) should be set up and checked, so that vocalists, flautists, violinists, etc. are not kept waiting unnecessarily.

Tuning up: A systematic approach can save time—keyboards first, guitars second, then any orchestral instruments.

* Unnecessary tension can arise when individuals who have already tuned up begin to play and talk while others are still trying to tune up. Help others to tune up.

* When one guitar has been tuned to the piano, the other guitarists can take that guitar into another room and tune to it, while other instruments tune to the piano.

* Maybe the musicians (or the church) could invest in a guitar-tuner. Tuning instruments by ear can be deceptively inaccurate. Tuners can also save time (especially for twelve-string guitars). An adequate model would

cost £25–35.

A devotional time: Three to four minutes, perhaps, led by a different person each time.

Spontaneous praise: Warm up with a few songs which don't need rehearsal, or use one of the exercises on pages 131–132 which will enable both singers and musicians to 'jam'. This can help you to relax and you'll find that rehearsals can be fun!

A time of sharing: Deal with any heaviness *before* the meeting. Unless inner pressures are resolved, leading will feel like wading through treacle. True worship embraces honesty and therefore we should try to unload any excess baggage onto the shoulders of the group. Music which issues from a caring atmosphere will have a greater depth.

Praying for the meeting: The theme should already be known. Seek God for any elements which he wants incorporated (words of knowledge, Scripture readings, specific aims, etc.)

Practice: Draw out each other's gifts. Don't be pushy. Eradicate the competitive spirit.

* Listen sensitively to each other. Don't just assume that you know what others are going to say. If someone is making a point, don't carry on quietly playing your instrument. No one should have to raise their voice to be heard.

* Aim to play by touch, not by sight. Many musicians feel inhibited in worship because their concentration is *totally* on the music book. It's hard to give your attention to two things at once. For most musicians, learning a whole repertoire off by heart would be impossible, but if at least an attempt could be made to commit a few songs to memory, this ability would breed more ability. Without this breakthrough, some musicians will always be stuck to the dots.

'Live' practice: When you are confronted with the people you're leading, areas which were glossed over in rehearsal become apparent. The stresses and strains of the live situation will detect any poor welding. Such pressures as remembering the words of the song you're singing, being aware of a difficult bar chord coming up, sensing which song would be right to sing next, introducing that song, setting the correct tempo, making sure your capo is on the right fret and so on, can all combine to reveal any practice which was threadbare.

* Nerves which lay dormant in rehearsal tend to be activated in a meeting. Anticipate how your material and presentation will fare when you are nervous.

* Record your talking, singing and playing. If you are not satisfied, the congregation is unlikely to be. *Think live!*

* Practise in the same way that you'll play in the meeting.

(a) The same place (building). A vicar once told me that each Saturday evening he'd go into the empty church building and preach the next day's sermon. I'm sure this helped him to deliver his material more confidently. When we have acclimatized ourselves to the place, it will be one less psychological barrier to overcome.

(b) The same position (stage-craft). If you're in a group, know where you'll position yourselves. If there are four vocalists and only one microphone, you could find yourselves jostling for position because you haven't run through who is standing where in relation to the microphone. (When one person is addressing the congregation, it is surprising how the movements of others at the front can detract from what is being said.)

(c) The same proximity (closeness). *Musicians* need to have good visual contact between each other—particularly between each section of the band. The rhythm section (keyboards, guitars and percussion) should be near to each other to help produce a 'tighter' sound. If a guitarist is taking the lead rhythmically, the percussionist needs to be near the guitar to synchronize with its accents. This applies especially to buildings where there is a delayed echo and you are apt to hear last week's service coming back at you!

There also needs to be visual contact between *musicians and leader(s)*. If, for example, the pianist (seated) is behind the vocalists (standing), the worship leader's cues (whether facial or by hand) will be ineffective. Don't rely on a vocal lead only.

(d) The same projection (volume). Practice, by its very nature, is a habit-forming activity. That is why a guitarist who strums quietly in rehearsal is likely to strum quietly in the meeting. We tend to tailor the volume of our playing to the size of the room in which we practise. If we rehearse in one place at one volume, then adjusting to another place at another volume will minimize effectiveness. An actor rehearsing the proclamation, 'Friends, Romans, Countrymen—lend me your ears!' must rehearse it in the style in which it is to be delivered. Our presentation will reflect the way in which we have practised.

(e) The same PA (amplification). If you use amplification in the meeting, use it in rehearsal. It's essential that musicians can hear both themselves and each other. Your success as a unit (as opposed to a group of individuals) will be determined by how mutually interdependent the members are as they play. Musicians need to be as dependent as two tightrope walkers—resonating and reaction with each other's playing. This can't happen if there is difficulty in hearing what others are playing.

In one church, the mid-week rehearsal takes place in a house where no amplification is used. The lead guitarist plays an acoustic guitar and the drummer plays on rubber practice pads. Everyone can hear each other. As a result, the flute and piano play each other off very creatively. But then comes the Sunday afternoon rehearsal in the church building, when apart from the drums all instruments and voices are amplified. The pianist now can't hear the flute very well because the lead guitar and the vocals are being drowned by the drums. The drummer is playing as quietly as possible but the acoustics of the large, echoey building are playing havoc with the slightest sound. The 'chemistry' between the musicians has broken down because of the sudden introduction of amplification. These problems could have been sorted out if the rehearsal had taken place under the same conditions.

Some suggestions concerning equipment: A Cobra 90 combo has six inputs. You can use a few microphones, guitars or keyboards through it. It is about £250–300. The Cobra 45 combo has three inputs and is £150–200. A good vocal microphone is the Bayer M69 for about £85 or the SM58 for £120.

(f) The same posture (sitting or standing). Generally speaking, if you stand to play your instrument in the meeting, practise in the same way. Otherwise a false sense of security can be created. For example, a below-average guitarist will find bar chords more difficult when standing because of the change in arm and wrist positions.

Worship: Use some of the songs you've just rehearsed. Let them run from one to another without a break.

Finish: If you set a time to end, keep to it.

Pack up: Everyone should help to either lift equipment or tidy up the practice area, so that no one is left to do it alone.

Part Three

In the Meeting

10

The Functions of A Worship Leader

1. To bring people to a place of worship

As we look at the following patterns of biblical worship, it must be remembered that entering the presence of God is not achieved through a *formula*.

The tabernacle

The main scriptural design for coming to God was that of the tabernacle. It can also be helpful for us to look at the procedure followed.

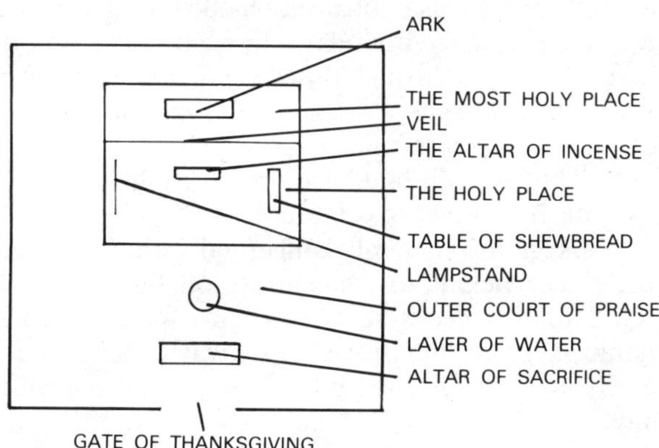

(a) The *outer court* represents the *body* of man where *thanksgiving* takes place for what God *has done*.

(b) The *Holy Place* represents the *soul* of man where *praise* takes place for what God *is doing*.

(c) The *Most Holy Place* represents the *spirit* of man where *worship* takes place for *who God is*.

Encamped—outside the tabernacle. How should we come before the Lord? 'Come before him with *joyful songs*' (Ps 100:2, NIV). The leader's role is to use such songs to rally the people for worship. He should be trying to bring people's hearts and minds together. This sense of unity can be helped by using songs that people can identify with—songs which speak of their own experience of God e.g. *I'm forgiven* and *Rejoice, Christ is in you*. These songs help the leader to gather the people's individual thoughts and focus them on God. When this sense of oneness is emerging, the people can be led on further, but not until then.

The Hebrews understood that moving into the presence of God had to be done by degrees. The psalms of ascent (Ps 120–134) which they sang on feast days while journeying to Jerusalem reminded them of this. These psalms begin with man *petitioning* God (Ps 120:1) and ending with man *blessing* God (Ps 134:2). The songs moved them from an awareness of their problems to an awareness of his presence.

Enter his gates with thanksgiving. The altar of sacrifice was the first object the worshipper came across. This speaks of the offering of our bodies as a living sacrifice (Rom 12:1). Our bodies must be surrendered to God before they can become vehicles of thanksgiving. The Hebrew meaning of 'thanksgiving' is 'to revere with extended hands'. Thanksgiving will often involve clapping, dancing and joyful shouting.

The second object was the laver of water which speaks of the word washing us (Eph 5:26). Use songs of thanksgiving which are centred around the word. Thanksgiving relates to what God has *done*. Use such songs to move the people through this stage of your approach.

Enter his courts with praise. Praise is the only means of entry to the presence of God. To praise meant to sing 'halals' (the root word for 'hallelujahs'). This is translated 'to make a show, to boast, to be clamorously foolish, to rave, to celebrate'.

Whereas thanksgiving is mainly concerned with *things* that have been done for us, praise begins to concentrate on the *person* doing them. Thanking God for his *deeds* should produce praise for his *character*. Songs of thanksgiving for the *past* will give way to songs of praise for the *present*. Once songs of praise are being sung, don't reintroduce songs of thanksgiving.

The leader should not say too much, and resist making tenuous links. It takes much longer to move the people into *worship*, than it does to move them into *praise*, because there is a need for various aspects of a person's being to be dealt with: the sacrifice of wills, the illuminating of minds and the release of emotions, represented by the table of shewbread, golden lampstand and altar of incense respectively.

Enter the Most Holy Place. Thanksgiving and praise have been preparing us for worship by causing our bodies, wills and emotions to be yielded to God. Psalm 95 points to the necessity of these preparatory stages. 'Come, let us sing to the Lord; let us make a joyful noise...' (v.1). 'Let us come into his presence with *thanksgiving*; let us make a joyful noise to him with songs of *praise*!' (v.2). Then we read, 'O come, let us *worship* and bow down, let us kneel before the Lord, our Maker' (v.6). Psalm 96 further underlines this progression: 'Great is the Lord, and greatly to be *praised*' (v.4); 'Come into his courts' (v.8); '*Worship* the Lord in holy array' (v.9).

We must not try to pre-empt the moment when worship begins. Just because we've sung our four songs of praise it doesn't mean it's time to sing *Within the veil*. It's often a slow transition from praise to worship; from focusing on God's blessings to God himself. Having said that, we can engage in an unnecessary excess of praise songs in the outer court, when really the people are ready to worship. The leader needs sensitivity to move the people further into God's presence. Failure to accomplish this can often be due to there being no plan to the overall worship in the time allocated.

Following the pattern of the tabernacle, to which Psalm 100 refers, our aim is 'to bless his name' (v.4). Having come inside the veil into the Most Holy Place, care must be taken by the leader:

* not to pull people back out to the gate of thanksgiving with an exuberant, rhythmic song (unless it's the final song);
* to allow the people to bathe in God's presence;
* to allow maybe just a few songs to be sung—repeated to act as channels for worship;
* not to disturb the worship with unnecessary talking;
* to trust the people with silence;
* to conclude the worship sensitively. This depends on whether the worship has culminated in gifts of the Spirit, healing, an altar call or a hush.

Conclusion: *Worship takes time*. (Does the clock always rule?)

2. To give strong leadership

People need to feel secure—you have to grant them this. You need to 'perform' as well as you can. At times, a leader will appear like a swan: all calm and serene on the surface but paddling like mad underneath!

Manner: Don't assume a sophisticated or 'religious' air.

Body: Relax. Over-compensate for nervousness or timidity. Don't stand woodenly or hide behind a music stand.

Face: Don't allow the microphone to obstruct the congregation's view of your face.

Eyes: Regard the congregation as individuals, not as blobs. Look at them. Don't avoid eye contact.

Mouth: Don't speak too much (worship leaders generally do). Avoid jargon—not everyone may know what is going on. Don't speak in an affected tone of voice. Speak up—always speak to the person on the back row—and speak slowly (we tend to speak faster when nervous).

Hands: Don't play with the microphone while talking.

Distracting mannerisms: Ask yourself, or even better someone else, whether you have any irritating habits which cause people's stress level to rise. Do you help people to unwind or do you wind them up? Do these habits inadvertently draw people's attention away from the Lord to yourself?

3. To minister to the Lord

(See also *Praise the Lord! Why?*)

'The Lord has chosen you to stand in his presence, to minister to him' (2 Chron 29:11). God created us to be worshippers first and workers second. We mustn't reverse that order. Society determines what you *are* by what you *do*. Achievement equals worth.

Sometimes our worship can be tainted by the world's philosophies. In some churches, worship is a means of quietening people down as they come in, or a convenient way of getting from the collection to the lesson, or the preliminaries before the preaching. In other churches, people are so preoccupied with the gifts of the Spirit or signs and wonders (vital as they are), that they're forgetting *just to worship God*—and to do it in such a way that makes him want to join in.

4. To minister to the people

There are all sorts of moods, temperaments and musical tastes represented. Some may be full of get-up-and-go, while for others all their get-up-and-go has got-up-and-gone. Some will be on spiritual mountain tops, going on with God and experiencing God's forgiveness, while others are in the doldrums, backsliding into secret sin.

Ministry means enabling the people to express themselves to God. This depends on (a) the leader's character, sensitivity to the Holy Spirit and musical skill; (b) the people's awareness of their responsibility to come prepared and ready to participate. 'Responsibility' means 'responsive ability'—the ability to respond maturely.

5. To motivate the people to praise

Help them to begin to communicate with God. This includes those who are tired, apathetic, ill, obstinate or hurting. We have to enable them to give of their best. When Abraham worshipped (Gen 22:16–17), he withheld nothing. David would not give God that which cost him nothing (2 Sam 24:24).

6. To help the people to hear from God

Is your worship a monologue or a dialogue? Worship for some people can be like speaking to someone on the telephone and feeling unsure if there is actually anyone on the other end of the line. This is often the case because *we* do all the talking! God made us with the capacity to listen and speak. He dropped a big hint as to which was the most important by equipping us with twice as many ears as mouths! If worship is to be likened to a telephone conversation, then from our point of view it will involve us talking, but we have to listen as well.

God speaks in all kinds of different ways: his word, other Christians, divine 'coincidences', dreams, etc. He also speaks through the means laid down in 1 Corinthians 12:8–11. The gifts of the Holy Spirit are given by God to enable us to help each other. As we are open to being used in such ways, we fulfil this purpose.

The phrase 'freedom in the Spirit' for many has meant *their* freedom instead of *Jesus'* freedom to say and do what *he* wants. Our failure to give him the opportunity to speak has restricted the healing he is waiting to bring us. Our meetings can easily become a hive of activity packed into one hour, with little sense of God having responded to us at the end.

7. To help the people to share what God is saying

You might find it helpful as a fellowship to ask yourselves these questions:

(a) To what extent does 1 Corinthians 14:26–33, 39–40 mirror our experience together?

(b) When we meet together, how can we make provision for God's building up of the body of Christ through the gifts he has ordained in 1 Corinthians 12:8–11?

(c) What misunderstandings and fears hinder us from 'earnestly desiring spiritual gifts' (1 Cor 14:1)?

(d) Do we encourage more than the same few people to share?

(e) Are we getting stuck in a rut with the same types of gifts?

Each individual has a duty not to come empty handed but to come as prepared as the speaker and musicians (1 Cor 14:26). Through the various contributions, the overall picture of what God is communicating can emerge. Each person must realize their responsibility for their section of the picture. The role of leader is not to dictate but to enable responsiveness to God. No one has got it together, but together we've got it!

8. To help the people to respond to what God is saying

People may have come looking forward to a time of celebration, but if God is evidently telling them to repent, they must do it! God means what he says. Don't cover up with 'cosmetic worship'—dancing, clapping, etc. It may even be right to leave the people in a spirit of repentance (not condemnation). Don't just tag on a few joyful songs to lighten the atmosphere. You may be relieving people from heaviness but, in so doing, evading reality.

Similarly, if God leads you into a time of celebration, don't think that after singing a few lively songs a number of times through you should then move on. God wants us to dig deep into each rich vein of truth he leads us to. He wants worship to be an *experience*, not just an *exercise*.

9. To help the people to absorb what God is saying

The reason for singing is to allow the meaning of a song to become real to us. Meaningful repetition can help the truths to penetrate further and further into our being, until our spirit is coated with them.

God may lead us to concentrate on one particular facet of his word for weeks or even months, reiterating it until it is being fleshed out in us. We may find ourselves picking up on a theme that we thought we'd finished with the previous week if God feels we are not believing or implementing what he says.

10. To help the people to explore what God is saying

Each meeting needs to be flexible enough so that we not only have time to move into areas God wants us in, but also to *explore* them. If the clock rules, we may be in danger of having to stop just when we're getting somewhere. Leading can sometimes be like navigating a yacht. It takes time to get your bearings right and for the sails of people's expectancy to be raised.

So often, having entered God's presence, we can be like people who call in for a cup of tea but never have time to stay and deepen the relationship. God wants our times together to be nourishing as he shares himself with us.

11. To keep the worship on course

Each meeting is special to God. Being led by the Spirit means being guided to specific targets which God has prepared beforehand. Therefore, leading means leading the people *somewhere*. Sometimes a person may make a 'spanner in the works' contribution which causes us to deviate from our course. Getting back on course without making such people feel they're being thrown out of the boat requires sensitivity.

Most leaders can lead songs, but leading worship means co-operating with the Holy Spirit. It is neither you nor he who is leading—you are leading together.

12. To correct any habit patterns

Let the worship ebb and flow. Just because there is a silence after a surge of worship doesn't mean there won't be another wave.

Don't let things become predictable. For instance, in many churches the mystery seems to have gone from singing in tongues because of its almost programmed occurrence and style. It should be able to occur many times in a meeting, varying in length, rising and falling in contour and changing in volume and intensity.

13. To direct and inspire the musicians

Encourage them to blend together as a unit. Help them to listen to and play off each other. Individuals can easily get locked into their own part. Don't be afraid to direct them openly: 'Just the piano'; 'Without the guitars'; etc. Be prepared to stimulate them to sing or play prophetically. The Levites 'prophesied under the direction of the king' (1 Chron 25:2). Of course, this requires skill as well as spiritual depth in your musicians.

14. To prepare people for the preaching (or to encourage a response to it)

The worship should flow into (or out of) the preaching. They must dovetail. If the word has been about repentance, we must be prepared to abandon our plans to celebrate. Alternatively, if it calls for rejoicing, even having had a time of celebration earlier shouldn't negate the possibility of another. The musicians must be prepared for more than one block of worship.

11

Lift Off

Here are some points to bear in mind as the meeting progresses.

1. Last minute check

Tuning, plectrums, capos, reeds, sticks, mutes, song numbers, OHP acetates, etc.

2. Musicians pray with leadership

3. Ten minutes before the meeting

Musicians play through some of the songs they'll be using in the meeting. This creates a worshipful environment. The people coming in should be encouraged to sing (seated). This time will help the musicians to relax and worship. Many music groups do very little worship in their rehearsals—it tends to be mostly practice—so this brief time will prepare them for later. The musicians can sometimes be waiting a long time in a meeting before they are required to play, so this should help to get the engine revved up.

4. As the meeting starts

Start with a few songs. Get people to stand.

5. Notices

6. Teach any new songs

7. Continue with the rest of the meeting

Don't use songs as polyfiller between other elements of the meeting, e.g. hymns, collection, song, reading, song, etc. This can cause a meeting to lurch along.

Have a block time of worship. Apart from avoiding any unnecessary breaks, the music acts as a bridge to help us get from self, leader, or people-consciousness to God-consciousness.

8. Pray

At the beginning of this time, ask for the protection of Jesus' blood over each person and for the worship to have an impact on their lives. Like a champagne bottle being broken at a ship's launch, or a gun being fired at the start of a race, this prayer should signal the commencement of a time of meaning business with God. (You might also ask a few people to pray briefly. Right at the outset, this can be corporate worship.)

9. Announce the title and number of the song

Yes, incredibly basic but some music groups start playing the introduction to their song and the congregation are left to play 'spot the chorus'. Don't create uncertainty in the people.

10. Food for thought

People's minds can be busy and cluttered as they come into a meeting. A few helpful words can displace things which might eclipse their view of God and act as a springboard for thoughtful worship. For example, before the song *Bless the Lord, O my soul* (SOF no.43), you might say, 'The Scriptures tell us to bless the Lord. They wouldn't do so unless God could be blessed. Yes, God can be blessed, roused, thrilled, ministered to and can experience pleasure as a result of our praises. So now, let's do just that—bless him, letting "all that is within me bless his holy name".'

If you are introducing the worship be:

(a) Prepared. Plan beforehand. I'm all for spontaneity, but unless you have a flare for this, your off-the-cuff remarks designed to stir people's hearts could end up as shapeless waffle, causing their cringe-factor to rise instead.

(b) Brief. There's no need for a lot of background information. People don't need to know whether the author was facing south-west when he wrote the song!

(c) Sensitive. Even if you have spent time preparing pearls of wisdom to share during the worship, be prepared not to raise them should they seem irrelevant at the time. There's no point in drawing attention to truth which is inconsequential. Also, base what you say on the Lord, not on yourself.

(d) Gentle. If you are not the minister, don't act as if you are. Know where your responsibilities begin and end. Don't reprimand the people.

11. Tell the people to stand

The quality and volume of singing is improved when people are standing. It also aids concentration. State it graciously, don't suggest it timidly. Say that as the worship continues they should feel free to sit, stand, kneel, etc.

12. Instrumental introduction

Guitarists should ensure that capos are in place *before* the song is introduced, otherwise it can delay the proceedings momentarily. Worse still is starting a song with the capo in the wrong place. Introductions should be:

(a) Played by one person. This saves having a count-in. It also avoids the dissonance created by one musician playing D-G-D-A for an introduction while another plays D-A-G-D.

(b) Rehearsed. The rehearsing of any song can be so concentrated on the actual song that the introduction is neglected. As part of making people feel they are in capable hands, have well-defined introductions so that no one is left in doubt as to when the introduction is over and when they are required to sing.

(c) Brief. Attempting to play an introduction in the meeting without having rehearsed one can result in the whole song being played because the musician can't find a convenient place to stop.

Introductions should be either four or eight bars in length.

Example 3: Here is a guitarist's introduction for the song *When the Spirit of the Lord* (SOF no.604):

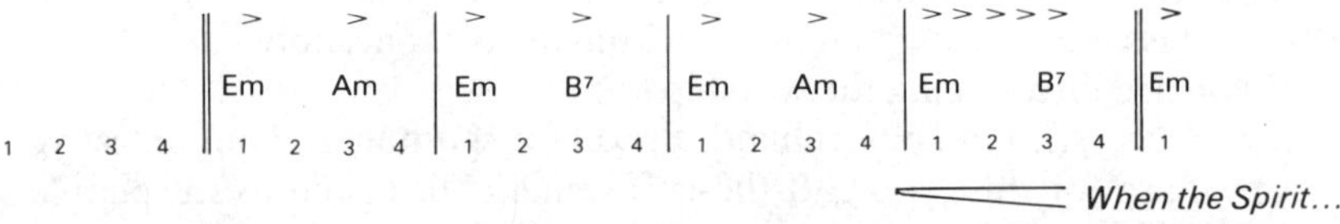

(d) Well accented. A common unsettling occurrence is when a musician plays the opening chord and immediately starts singing, expecting everyone to sing in time. This causes a tug-of-war between musicians and congregation as each tries to assert its own rhythm. So, set a regular pulse which prepares people to sing together. Musicians can't overemphasize the accents enough in the introductions.

(e) Confident. If the introduction is played timidly, the singing is likely to begin timidly. Start as you mean to go on.

(f) Interesting. In any piece of music you listen to, the most important time in formulating your positive or negative reaction to it will be in the first ten seconds. A confident, thoughtful introduction can help to draw a more immediate response out of people, rather than having to use the first verse as a time for 'stoking the fire' to get them warmed up.

Example 4: For I'm building a people of power (SOF no.109). The introduction is D-G-D-A^7, but the A^7 chord has been embellished.

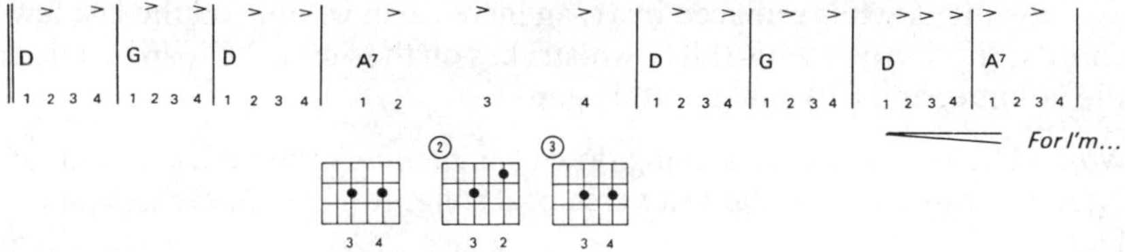

(The numbers ② and ③ refer to the fret number.)

Example 5: Another decorated introduction using simple chords to the song *I will sing unto the Lord* (SOF no.267).

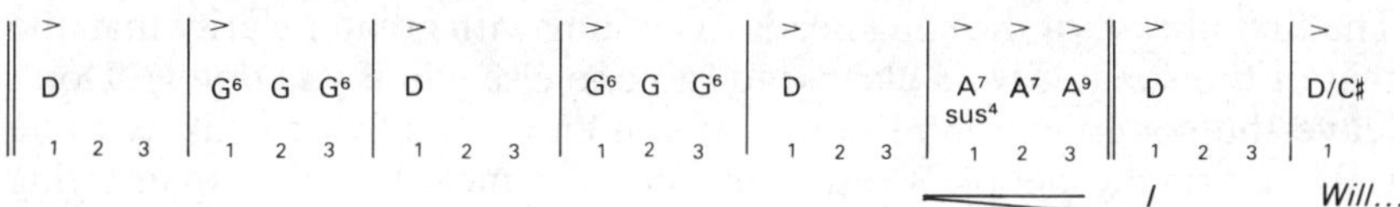

Chords used in an introduction should be centred around I, IV and V. For an example in the key of D, this means using D(I), G(IV) and A(V).

Pianists need to be able to locate quickly which sections of a song's melody should be used as a brief introduction.

Example 6: Here is an introduction for *Majesty* (SOF no.358).

(g) Not slowing down. Many musicians slow their introductions down just before the singing commences. This seems nonsensical, because part of the aim of the introduction is to set a tempo for everyone to sing in time with. If you then slow down, the original tempo has to be restated. A better solution to helping people know where the introduction ends and where the singing starts, is illustrated here in the song *I love You, Lord* (SOF no.203).

Example 7:

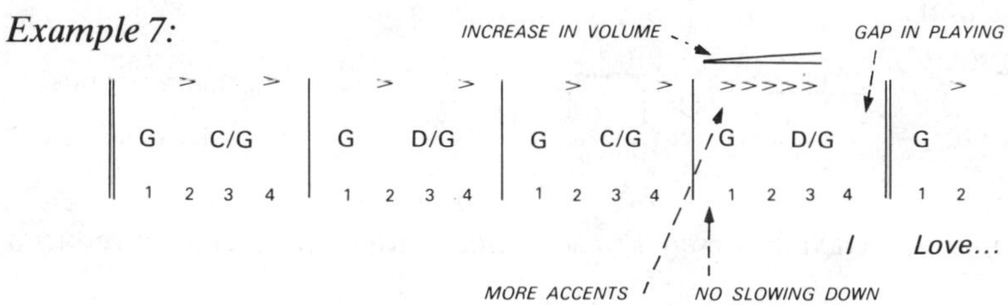

So, slowing down is replaced by (i) an increase in volume on the last few chords; (ii) more accents (all down-strokes on the guitar) to help increase the volume, and (iii) a momentary gap.

Note: The technique of slowing down (or *ritenuto*) can be used to great effect as you come to the last verse of a song, to give a more grandiose feel.

Summing up: Make sure introductions are played by one person, rehearsed, brief, well accented, played confidently, interesting and not slowed down.

13. Lead the singing in

The first phrase of the song needs to be sung with greater clarity than the rest of the song. Give a clear lead (no one else will if you don't). Don't leave the congregation in doubt. If you enter timidly, it is likely to be reflected in the people's response. Sing the melody rather than trying harmonies, though the other singers in the group should use harmonies, encouraging the congregation to also.

14. Singing and playing simultaneously

If you find the combination of singing and maintaining steady accents difficult, at least try to sing the first phrases of each important section of the song, and then return to concentrating on your playing. If you don't at least do this, people will not be clear merely from your instrumental introduction where they are supposed to come in. Once you have brought them in with a vocal lead, you don't have to keep singing as they should be able to carry the tune.

Inexperienced guitarists can make their task of leading songs more difficult by playing complicated strumming patterns. Many of the strokes in a pattern can be omitted without losing the feel of the song. The main feature of strumming should be its *regular accents*, so you can afford to edit strumming to its bare essentials.

Example 8: With strumming for *Ah, Lord God* (SOF no.3) the *Teach Yourself Praise Guitar* pattern no.1 can be reduced from

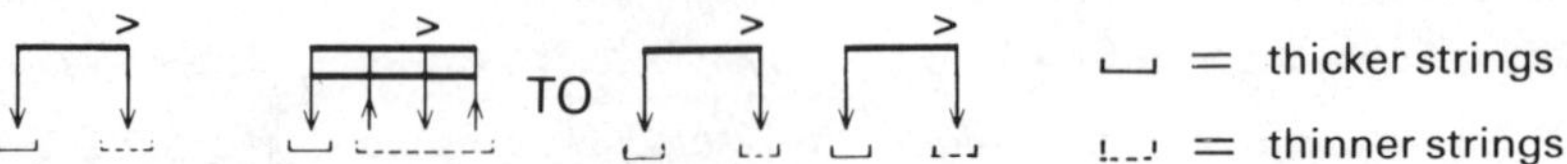

Example 9: Teach Yourself Praise Guitar pattern no.2 can be reduced from

for *I just want to praise You* (SOF no.199).

15. Speaking and playing simultaneously

Learn how to give instructions between verses, such as, 'Just voices'; 'Just the musicians'; 'Last time'; etc. without losing tempo or playing the wrong chords. This needs practice. Isolate such areas and become fluent in them. Speak with extra clarity and volume so that no one is left in doubt. Be decisive. Don't be over-modest. Make the phrase fit in.

Example 10: If having sung the song a few times through, both musicians and congregation are unsure as to whether another verse follows, make a clear and early direction to avoid hesitancy, as in this example of *I will sing unto the Lord* (SOF no.267).

...praise ye the	*Lord*	*"And again,*	*I will sing"*		*I*	*will...*
A^7	D	G	D	A^7	D	D/C♯
>	>	>	>	> > >	>	>
1 2 3	1 2 3	1 2 3	1 2 3	1 2 3	1 2 3	1 2 3

Note: When making announcements, drop the volume of the playing so that people can hear. Then raise it as you come to the verse.

If you want everyone to sing a particular verse softly, this needs stating. For example, in the song *In my life, Lord* (SOF no.216) one of the verses might be, 'In my *thoughts*, Lord.' In the gap before that verse, you would say, 'In my thoughts, softly,' while dropping the volume of the music and keeping it low during that verse.

Summing up: (i) drop volume of music; (ii) announce clearly; (iii) resume (or lower) volume; (iv) increase accents; (v) lead singing back in confidently.

16. Keep the worship flowing

You can break the flow with too much talking, and introductions to songs can become like adverts during a film. 'Guard your steps when you go to the house of God... let your words be few' (Eccles 5:1–2).

17. *Avoiding the hiccups*

To avoid the worship becoming stilted after each song, let the musicians continue to play very softly on one chord or sequence, as illustrated below:

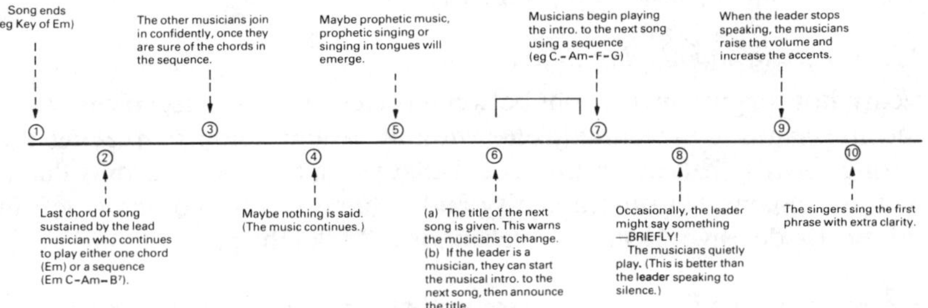

Note: The technique of laying down a soft carpet of music between songs is best suited to quiet worship rather than boisterous praise.

Example 11: (The numbers ①,② etc. correlate with the number in the diagram above.)
Song 1: *Holy is the Lord* (SOF no.170—key Em). Song 2: *Holy is the Lord of hosts* (SOF no.167—key C).

Note: Any chord sequences should be established by the lead musician. When the others have identified the chords in the sequence, they can join in.

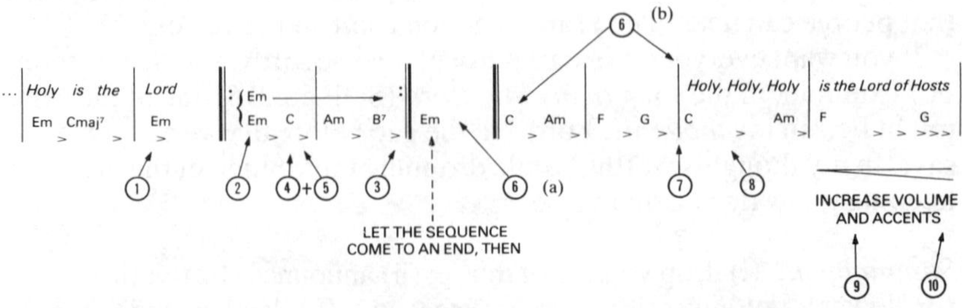

18. *Smoothing out the wrinkles*

If people have been standing for a while, to suddenly ask them to sit can be taken by some to be a signal for the preaching; hence the emergence of a wave of coughing and rustling. To eradicate this you could say, 'Continuing in that worshipful attitude, let's sit as we sing number twenty....'

19. Have any ministry separate

Sometimes the singing has no sooner begun, than prayers, gifts of the Holy Spirit, etc. start to emerge from the congregation. It is best if there is a concentrated time of singing to God before we move into other areas. During a time of ministry, there may come a prophetic song which inspires further worship, but again watch that different aspects of the worship don't break the continuity.

20. Yo-yo worship

Avoid the situation where, having sung for a while, you ask people to sit, only to realize that the next song you feel should be sung is an up-tempo one for which you want people to stand. Generally have blocks of time where people stand then sit, although people should feel free to sit when others are standing and vice versa.

21. Stillness

If there appears to be unnecessary movement which could be a distraction to others, ask people to be still for a moment. Help people to learn how to relate to the presence of God.

22. Closed eyes

Sometimes people fail to enter into worship because of external distractions. Casually encouraging people to feel free to close their eyes can be a helpful aid to them focusing on God.

12

Creativity in Worship

Variety—the spice of life

The following ideas have no spiritual value in themselves, they are merely aids to worship. They are not to be used for their own sake, as tricks up your sleeve or as ornamental extras, but rather as an integral part of your worship expression. Though they can help to prevent songs becoming dull and predictable and guard against mindless repetition, their main purpose is to state the message of the song more skilfully—underscoring, heightening and creating a deeper awareness of the meaning of the words, so that they have a greater impact on the singer. A new perspective can be given on well-worn songs.

There is little value in using my own ideas in parrot fashion. They are to be adapted for use with your own repertoire. Plan thoughtfully the use of these techniques prior to the worship. Be careful not to program your songs (e.g. second time—just instruments; third time—just voices, etc). Each idea must be a response to the worship at a given moment. Creativity must issue from an encounter with God.

If you are leading worship where few, if any, of the following variations have ever been used, don't suddenly incorporate them without first preparing the people. At the beginning of the worship you could say that there are many and various ways in which we can worship God (list a few of these ideas) and conclude by saying these are a small reflection of the variety and creativity of our God. People need helping through any reluctance to new ways of worshipping as this is sometimes due to lack of education or laziness.

Instructions for leaders and musicians

In the gap between one verse and the next, the musicians should drop the volume of their playing slightly so that they and the congregation can hear the leader's instructions (e.g. 'Just the instruments.'). This can be done as follows:

Guitarists—play half as many strokes (but still maintain the accents).
Keyboards—play half as many notes (chords of longer length).
Woodwind, brass, strings—stop playing.
Drums—stop playing quavers on the high-hat (but still maintain the beat).

Note: The following occur after the song has been sung a few times through.

1. Just the ladies

Instructing the ladies to sing while the men wait their turn can have the feel of a choir practice. Therefore, this technique must be used sparingly and meaningfully. If you instruct the ladies to sing a verse, don't automatically give the next verse to the men. Choose which songs would benefit most from this idea.

Example: Jesus, how lovely You are (SOF no.274). Just the ladies sing, 'Hallelujah! Jesus is pure and holy . . . ' The rest of the song is to be sung by everyone.

2. Just the men

The use of any idea is to enhance the words. Never instruct *just* the ladies or *just* the men to sing simply because you fear it might be tedious for them to sing it a number of times together.

Example: Jesus, Your love has melted my heart (SOF no.284). Have the men sing it once through, without the ladies doing the same. In an age where men often find it difficult to articulate the way they feel, encouraging the men alone to sing of the effect of the love of Jesus on their hearts and emotions can have great power. Indeed, at the end of one conference, someone told me that out of all the talks, seminars and times of worship, this had touched him the most. (Also: *Isn't He beautiful?* [SOF no.228].)

3. First the ladies, then the men (or vice versa)

Example: Worthy art Thou (SOF no.620). 'Worthy art Thou, O Lord our God' (L); 'For You are reigning...' (M); 'Jesus is Lord of all the earth' (T).

Example: Rejoice! (SOF no.461). 'God is at work in us' (L); 'Where things impossible' (M); 'Rejoice!' (T). (Also: SOF nos 343/358.)

4. Changing the words

(a) In the title: Constantly review your repertoire to see whether there is some way you can bring freshness to what may have become over-familiar words.

Example: Change the words of the song *Jesus, Your love has melted my heart* to 'Jesus, Your love *is* melting my heart.' There are always going to be people in a meeting for whom the words 'has melted' are simply not true. It might be best to start by singing 'is melting'. Before the song, you might even say, 'Let's allow the Spirit to come and thaw out those stony areas of our lives where we are hard of heart and touchy.' Then, as you come to the last time through, you could announce, 'Your love *has* melted my heart.' The musicians could reflect this change in words by raising the volume of their playing.

Example: I was in a prayer meeting where a lady asked for prayer because a certain relationship difficulty had brought her to the very brink of abandoning her faith in God. As we prayed for her, we sensed the Lord wanted to refresh her tired spirit. As part of our prayer, we sang *River, wash over me* (SOF no.468), changing the word 'me' to 'her'. This song could also be used when praying about situations where there is national or domestic unrest, singing, 'River, wash over them,' or 'it'.

Example: The words of the song *I will enter his gates* (SOF no.252) could be altered to 'I will enter my work, my home, my church, my school...'. Even at the risk of being somewhat trite and of altering the scriptural basis of the song, at least it might make us stop and think whether we really are entering our work, home, church or school with the kind of thanksgiving and praise in our hearts which will begin to transform those situations.

(b) In the verse or chorus:

Example: *Worthy art Thou* (SOF no.620). Change the words of the chorus, 'Jesus is Lord of all the earth,' to, 'Jesus is Lord of all my life.'

Example: *When the Spirit of the Lord* (SOF no.604). As well as 'sing', 'clap', 'praise' and 'dance' you could insert 'shout' and 'leap'. Also, a whole verse can be sung to 'la'.

5. In the singular and plural

Example: The song *He is Lord* (SOF no.159). This could be sung differently on each verse: 'He's our Lord'; 'You're my Lord'; 'You're our Lord.' You could vary it even further by omitting the accompaniment or playing it very softly when you come to sing, 'You're my Lord.' Apart from adding contrast, it would give a more personal, private touch. (Remember that as you come to that particular verse, you would have to announce, '"You're *my* Lord"—softly,' so that people capture the spirit in which it is to be sung.)

Example: The first time through the song *Father, we love You* (SOF no.98), the three verses could be sung in the singular: 'Father, *I* love You,' etc. Then you could sing them in the plural, which would give the worship a more corporate feel. (You might try raising the volume for these three verses.)

6. Ministering to one another

Below is an example of how a song can be used as a vehicle of that expression.

Example 12:

(a)

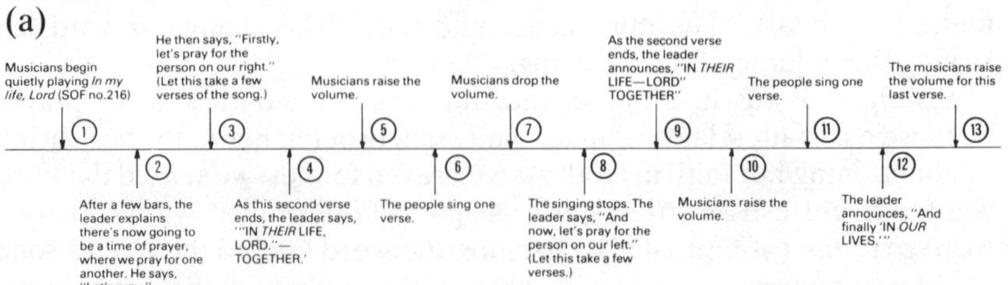

(b) You may feel it would be better to omit points 4 to 7. This would mean that the musicians would play very quietly as people prayed and the song would conclude the prayer time.

Other songs: SOF nos.468, 236, 337 and 'Spirit of the living God, fall afresh on *them*'?

Note: Sometimes, as a gesture of our concern for each other, suggest that people link hands.

7. Just the musicians

The problem: who takes the lead? Musicians must be ready to respond confidently when the worship leader suddenly announces, 'Just the musicians.' It's no good at that point for the flautist to drop a panic-stricken look at the pianist as if to say, 'Who plays the melody?' A problem that can arise is that the lead-line instrumentalists all hesitate out of a genuine sense of not wanting to be 'pushy'. In the end, they all miss the boat and the song lurches forward with the guitarists playing chords and the pianist hesitantly playing the melody. When leading worship, don't be over-modest.

The solution: lay down ground-rules. Before each meeting, the musicians must be clear about which instrument(s) will take the lead if the instruction 'Just the musicians' is given. If this direction was to be used on a *number* of songs, it would be best if the instrument taking the lead was different each time. For example, one time the clarinet; another time the piano.

Application: alternative instrument combinations. (a) The tunes of some songs such as *When I feel the touch* (SOF no.600) can be divided into two sections: instrument 1 (e.g. violin) plays section 1: 'When I feel... that I love You, Lord.' Instrument 2 (e.g. piano) plays section 2: 'So from deep... and I love You, Lord.'

(b) On the other hand, you may feel that instrument 1 should play the whole of the tune—especially for shorter songs such as *The steadfast love* (SOF no.541).

(c) Instrument 1 plays both sections; instrument 2 *joins in* at the second section.

(d) Instrument 1 plays the tune; instrument 2 plays 'answering phrases'.

Example 13: Emmanuel (SOF no.79).

(e) Both the instruments play *together*: instrument 1 plays the tune, instrument 2 plays a harmony.

Example 14: Open our eyes, Lord (SOF no.420).

(f) A combination of both (d) and (e).

Example 15: Majesty (SOF no.358).
Answering phrase

(g) Instrument 1 plays the tune; instrument 2 plays a 'counter-melody'.

Example 16: Worthy is the Lamb (SOF no.621).

Guidelines: (i) Musicians don't have to stick regimentally to the tune. A good player can sustain the main melody while decorating it with other melodic phrases. For example, *God of glory* (SOF no.136). (The asterisks mark the points where the main tune is picked out.)

(ii) If the worship leader says, 'Again, just the musicians,' then the instruments will have to be ready to play another verse. At this point, the approach explained in (i) would be helpful, especially if the tune has been played the first time.

(iii) In some situations, where there are a few instrumentalists who can improvise when the instruction 'just the musicians' is given, the song melody is in danger of disappearing because everyone is busy improvising. If your players are very sensitive and creative, this doesn't really matter so much, but for the majority of situations, it might be best if some instruments sustained the main tune while the others improvised.

(iv) After a verse or two of just the instruments playing, don't feel that you have to bring the congregation back in to sing. It may be right to let the musicians bring the song to an end.

8. Just the instruments (improvised playing)

Ministering to the people: There are incidents in the Scriptures where instrumental music clearly ministered to people. As we have already seen (in 1 Samuel 15–23), when King Saul was being tormented by an evil spirit the remedy for his oppression was a curious one. David was summoned to Saul's court, not to *pray* but to *play*. We are told that whenever David played his lyre the evil spirit left Saul, and he was refreshed. So, the incident occurred more than once. Therefore, it was not coincidental. We have to ask ourselves what God might be saying to us through such a passage and how we should implement the implications.

Planned spontaneity: There may be an appropriate moment in a meeting when you say to the people, 'I'm going to ask the musicians to minister to us right now.' Instead of playing the tune of a known song, the musicians could improvise—if necessary using chord sequences as a basis for their improvisation (see pages 128–129). The main requirement is a group of skilful musicians capable of producing music which will uplift the people. In preparation for such a moment, the rehearsals and worship prior to the meeting need to accommodate this. The lead-line instruments should join in after the chord sequence has been established by the rhythm section.

Example 17:

9. Just the voices (without the instruments)

This technique is best used with songs where your fellowship seems to naturally use harmonies. It isn't very effective with melodies sung in unison. The overall effect should be of different vocal lines weaving together a kind of musical tapestry. In order to prevent people feeling that the bottom of the song has suddenly dropped out, you will have to take a firmer grip on leading the song at that point, especially on the first phrase. To encourage people to launch out into singing harmonies and descants, begin singing this verse with a harmony line yourself.

Example 18: I love You, Lord (SOF no.203).

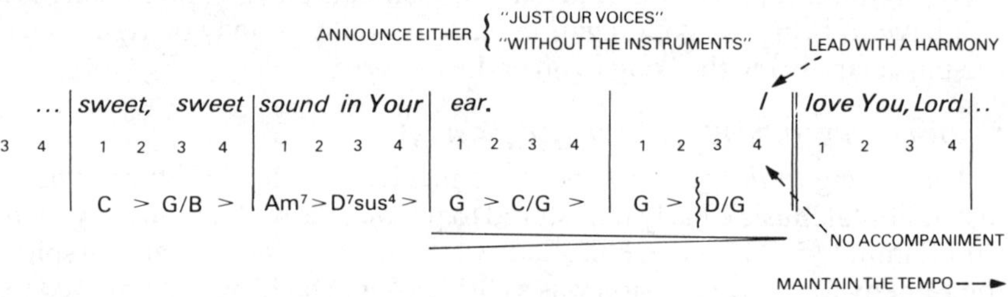

Important notes: (a) As you make the announcement for voices only, drop the volume of your playing.

(b) Lead the singing with a harmony.

(c) Since there is no instrumental accompaniment on the vocal verse, there will be a tendency for the tempo to drag. If this is only slight, it can be quite effective, but you need to beware that it can become too much like a dirge.

(d) It can be quite effective for this unaccompanied vocal verse to be the last verse of the song.

(e) If you are going to sing another verse with accompaniment, lead the singing in clearly (not a harmony line).

Example 19:

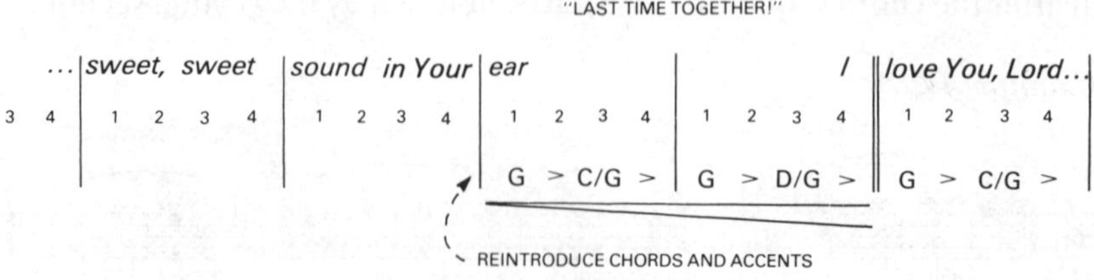

Example: He is Lord (SOF no.159). Before one of the verses announce, 'You're my Lord, just voices.'

Example 20: In the song *When the Spirit of the Lord* (SOF no.604), as the last chord dies away, announce, 'Just voices, when the Spirit of the

Lord is within my heart, I will *sing*.' It would be appropriate at this point to start singing a harmony line (a third above the main melody). There should be no prominent rhythm.

10. First section of song played by musicians; congregation entering at second

This variation can be applied to any song which has two contrasting sections. For example: SOF nos. 1, 39, 109, 147, 176, 189, 252, 274, 278, 312, 371, 531, 620, 630, 19, 112, 141, 149, 251, 337, 358, 471, 535 and 550.

Example 21: Father God (SOF no.92). Musicians play the section, 'Father God, I wonder....' The congregation join in at, 'I will sing Your praises...' The leader would have to say, 'I will sing...' the bar before that section, which would mean leaving out the last phrase of the verse to fit it in.

11. Humming

This is best done with songs that are: (a) worshipful and meditative; (b) not up-tempo; (c) pitched in the middle-range for voice; (d) not too lengthy.

Songs such as *Within the veil* would be suitable, but songs such as *I will enter His gates* should be avoided—unless you want to run the risk of people bursting blood vessels! In the gap before the verse where the humming will take place, announce, 'Let's hum the tune.' Don't just say, 'Hum.'

Some people find that singing 'ooh' is more comfortable than humming. To facilitate this, as you lead alternate between humming and oohing, so that others can follow.

The musicians should play very softly while people hum. Particular instruments may have to stop playing to re-enter in the next verse.

12. Whistling

This isn't something I would advise you ever actually to direct people to do. Everyone might just collapse into fits of laughter, or even worse, just to stand stony-faced. The best way to use it is when people are humming the tune or the musicians are playing a verse through without vocal accompaniment. As they do so, you might whistle either the tune, a harmony, or fragments of the tune. Be careful not to have your mouth too close to a microphone, though—it won't do a lot for people's ears, or their spirits!

13. Contrasting sections

(a) Volume—raising or lowering it: By creating areas of light and shade in a song, we can heighten the words so that people see them very differently.

Example 22: *Jesus, how lovely You are* (SOF no.274). Play the choruses softly and the verses loudly (except the verse beginning, 'Hallelujah! Jesus is meek and lowly....' Capture the sentiment of the words by playing it *softly*.) This is far better than the whole song being played at one volume. You could also strum the choruses and verses differently. The accents on the choruses could be on 2 and 4 whereas the strumming on the verses could be on 1, 2, 3 and 4 (as shown in the following diagram). In the gaps between choruses and verses, I would suggest you lead it as follows:

"HALLELUJAH!"

	...how	*lovely*	*You*	*are.*		*Hal* -	*le* -	*lu* -	*jah!*	*Je* -	*sus*	*is...*
3	4	1	2	3	4	1	2	3	4	1	2	3
		G^7		C		C		F		G		
	>		>	> > > >		>	>	>	>	>	>	>

Example 23: His Name is Wonderful (*Mission Praise* no.72). This can be broken down into three sections:

Section 1: 'His Name is Wonderful...' moderately loud.
Section 2: 'He's the Great Shepherd...' raise volume.
Section 3: 'Bow down before Him...' softly.

In the gap between the first two sections, to show that you wanted people to raise their voices as they sing 'He's the Great Shepherd', you would have to raise the volume of your playing and probably increase the number of accents as well at that point.

"...*Wonderful,*			*Je* -	*sus*	*my*	*Lord.*			*He's the Great*			*Shepherd*	*the*		*Rock*	*of*	*all..."*
1	2	3	1	2	3	1	2	3	1	2	3	1	2	3	1	2	3
B^7			A	E	B^7	E			B			B^7			E		
	>	>		>	>	> > > > > > >			>	>	>	> > > > > > >			>	>	>

INCREASE INCREASE

Note: Look at the accents. Notice how they are on 2 and 3 in the first section and 1, 2 and 3 in the second section. In the third section you could have the accents on 1 only to bring out phrases like 'bow down'.

Example: In the song *In my life, Lord* (SOF no.216), play verses such as 'In my thoughts' and 'On my lips' softly. The music will go part of the way towards drawing people's attention to such issues as their thought life and whether certain things they have said of late have been unhelpful or unnecessary. As a contrast, raise the volume for verses such as 'In our praise' and 'In our lives'.

Example 24: *Thank you, Jesus* (SOF no.500). The musical treatment should always mirror the mood of the words in each verse, so I suggest the following format: verse 1: 'Thank You, Jesus...' (moderately loud); verse 2: 'You went to Calvary...' (soft); verse 3: 'You rose up...' (loud).

(b) Rhythm—on the beat or off the beat:

Example 25: Peace I give to you (Graham Kendrick Song Book).
Section 1: 'Peace I give to you...' (softer—accents *on* the beat);
Section 2: 'Let it flow to one another...' (louder—accents *off* the beat).

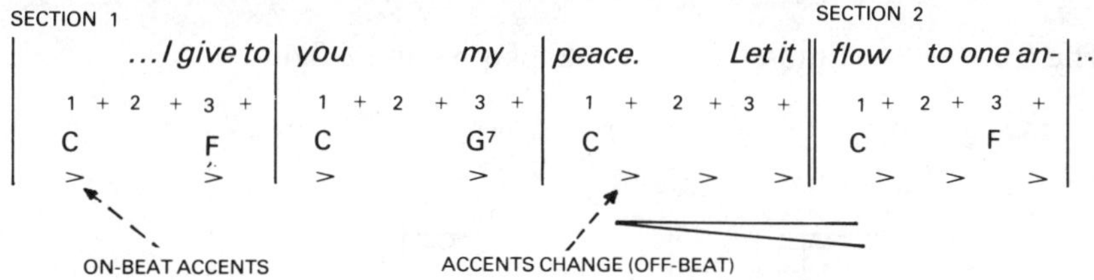

Note: Apart from the volume being raised in section 2, notice the change in the rhythmic pattern, with the accents now being on the *off-beat* (+). In section 1, they were beats 1 and 3. In the second section, the bass player and pianist's left hand would have to emphasize the beats 1, 2 and 3 while the pianist's right hand would take the off-beat accents, like this:

Example 26:

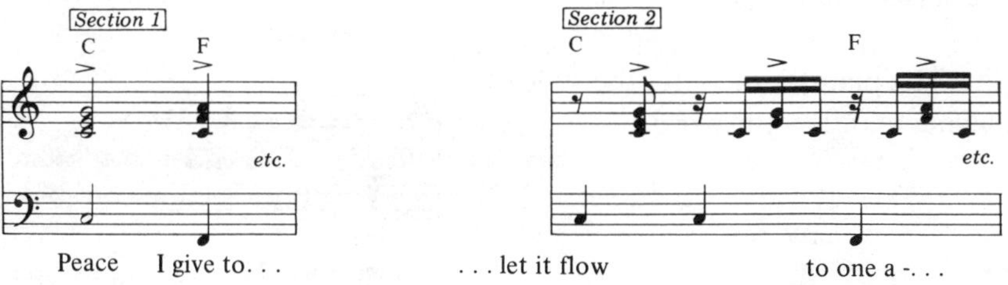

Note: These rhythms work best at a crisp pace.

Example 27: *I will call upon the Lord* (SOF no.251).
Section 1: 'I will call upon the Lord...' (half-tempo);
Section 2: 'The Lord liveth...' (double-time).

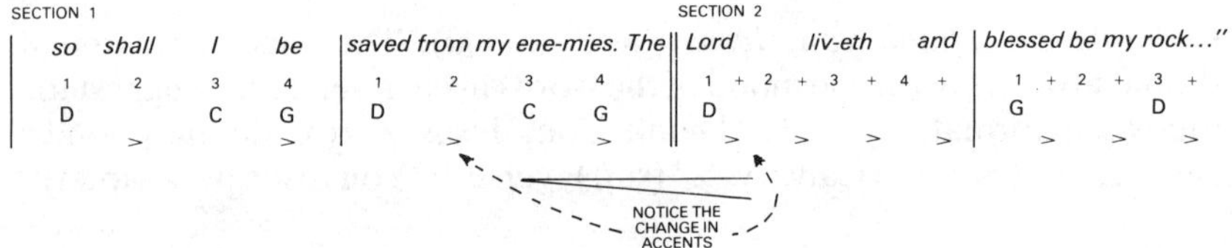

(c) Instrumentation—making a feature of particular instruments:

Example 28: Let's look again at the song, *Peace I give to you*. It continues with verses such as 'Joy I give to you', 'Love I give to you', etc. A verse such as '*Power* I give to you' could be treated differently in a number of ways.

(i) The guitar strumming could be much more dynamic, like this:

The trumpet (or flute/clarinet) could play a fanfare figure.

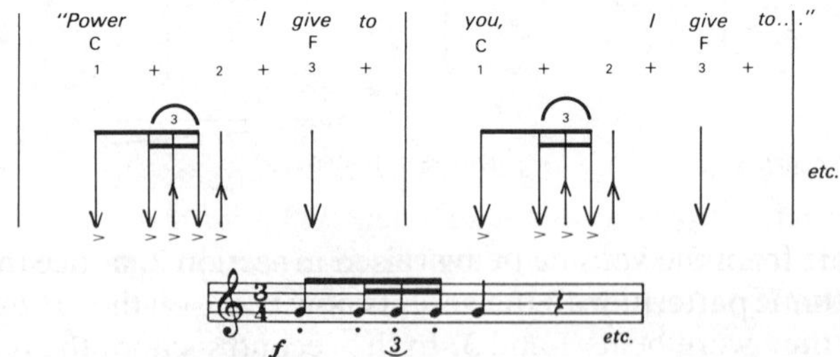

(ii) In the second section, the trumpet could continue the fanfare:

(iii) The piano could alter the style of playing to reflect the words.

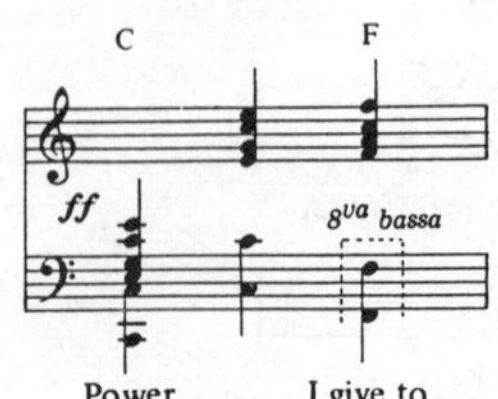

14. Highlighting particular lines

Example 29: *I love You, Lord* (SOF no.203).

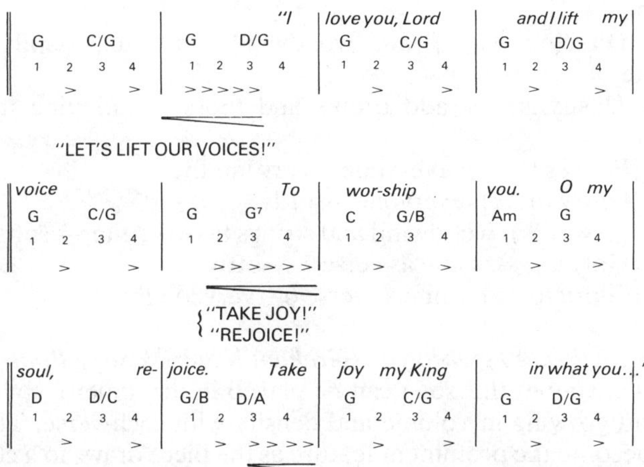

Here, the phrases 'lift my voice', 'O my soul, rejoice!' and 'take joy my King' are being highlighted. It would not be advisable to make this many announcements in one verse. (You're a worship leader not a bingo caller!) I've done it this way to show you the various possibilities.

Rhythmic development

Example 30: *Worthy is the Lamb* (SOF no.621). *Suggested rhythmic treatment*: The guitar should take the lead in building up this 'bolero' type rhythm. (If the musicians can't synchronize the rhythm, it is best left to one guitar and percussion.)

Suggested format:

Verse 1 (Worthy is...): guitar and bass—softly.
Verse 2 (Holy is...): second guitar, piano and cymbals—increasing volume.
Verse 3 (Precious is...): add woodwind and strings—still increasing volume.
Verse 4 (Jesus is...): add drums and brass—continuing to increase volume.
Verse 5 (Praises to...): everyone—very loudly.
Verse 6 (Glory to...): everyone—softly.
Verse 7 (no words): woodwind and strings take the tune—softly.
Verse 8 (Holy is...): same as verse 2—softly.
Verse 9 (Glory to...): same as verse 6—very loudly.

Example 31: Peace I give to you (Graham Kendrick Song Book). Like the previous example, this song can be played in the 'bolero' style, starting softly and growing in volume and density with each verse. The rhythm should become the prominent feature as the piece draws to a close.

16. Different tempos in a song

With careful and positive vocal and instrumental leading, a worship leader can further colour the fabric of a song by introducing different tempos.

Example 32: *Thank You, Jesus* (SOF no.500).

Suggested format:

Verse 1 (Thank You, Jesus): usual version played up-tempo and loud.
Verse 2 (You went to Calvary): usual version played up-tempo and moderately loud.
Verse 3 (You rose up from the grave): usual version, up-tempo and loud.
Verse 4 (You went to Calvary): new arrangement, slow and soft.
Verse 5 (same as verse 4).
Verse 6 (You rose up from the grave): usual version, up-tempo and loud.
Verse 7 (Thank You, Jesus): usual version, up-tempo and very loud.

The aim of changing tempo in a song is to dramatize the words. After singing this song, one person confessed that the truth of such conventional yet profound Christian statements as, 'You went to Calvary' and 'You rose up from the grave' hit him forcibly.

Execution: In terms of the mechanics of leading such an arrangement the problem areas are likely to come when setting new tempos. (In this example, between verses 3 and 4, and 5 and 6.) This needs to be led clearly and confidently.

Here is the end of the fourth verse leading into the new arrangement.

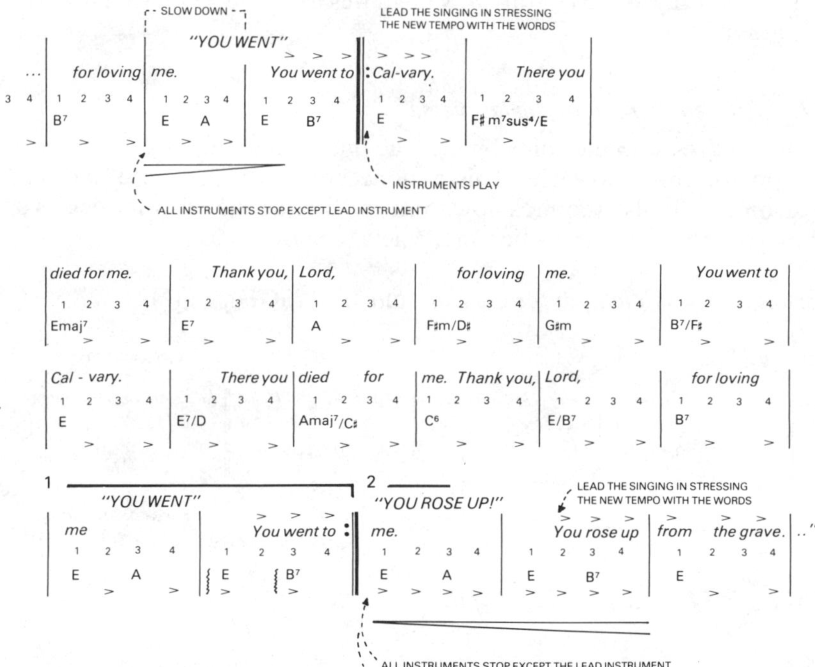

Main principles for other songs:

(a) One instrument should take the lead in setting the new tempo. This means all the instruments apart from the lead instrument need to stop at the same place. (In this example, this takes place on the word 'me' at the end of the fourth verse.)

(b) Over-emphasize the first few words of the verse in the new tempo. This will help to clarify the meter of this new tempo, so that both musicians and congregation are synchronized. (In this example, 'You went to Calvary...')

(c) You may feel that people are only beginning to relax into this slower verse as they come to the end of it. If so, direct them to sing it again by announcing, 'Again—"You went..."'

(d) At the end of the second time through this slower verse, make it clear to the other musicians that they should stop playing at the same place. (In this example, on the word 'me'.)

(e) The lead instrument should then firmly re-establish the original tempo.

(f) Bring the singing in, stressing the original tempo by over-emphasizing the first few words of this verse. (In this example, 'You rose up from the grave...')

17. Different tempo for the last verse

This requires strong leading by the lead musician to set a faster or slower tempo for this last verse. This is done both with the voice and lead instrument. It also requires 'togetherness' among the other musicians as they go through the transition in the new tempo.

Example 33: Hallelujah for the Lord our God (SOF no.147).

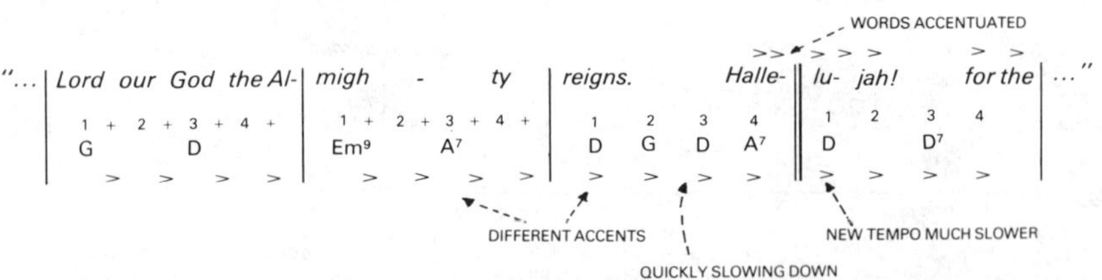

Example 34: When the Spirit of the Lord (SOF no.604).

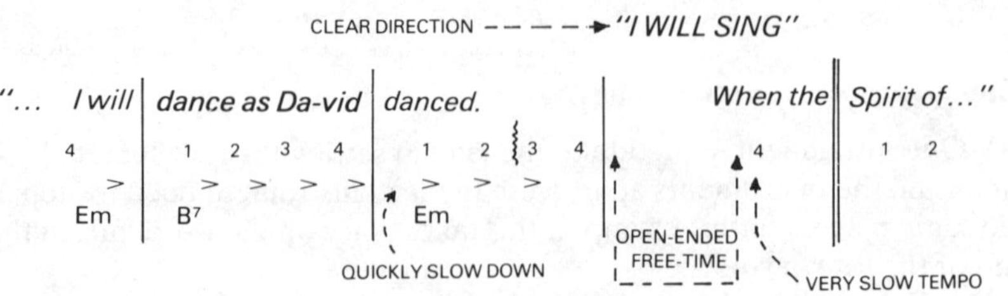

Alternatives

(a) Having slowed down, you could remain at that tempo for one verse and finish.

(b) The new tempo could gradually build up (as is often the case in songs of this kind).

(c) The first section of the new tempo could be sung unaccompanied. The musicians could enter at the section, 'I will sing.'

18. At half-tempo then full-tempo

Example 35: The song *Father, we love You* (SOF no.98), works well to two different rhythms.

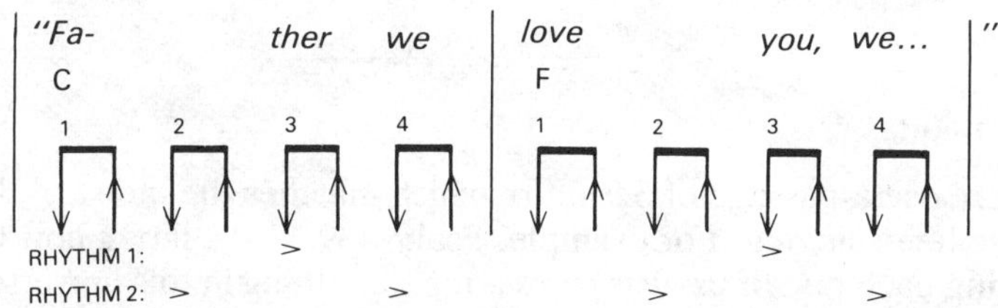

The accents in the first rhythm give a more relaxed feel to the song, whereas the second gives a more up-tempo feel to it. Both can be used in the same song with this suggested format:

'Father I love you'; 'Jesus I love you'; 'Spirit I love you' to rhythm 1; then 'Father *we* love you'; 'Jesus *we* love you'; 'Spirit *we* love you' to rhythm 2.

The change in tempo between verse 3 and 4 would have to be well practised, as would the announcement for the change in words to: 'Father *we* love you.'

Example 36: Rejoice! (SOF no.461). The choruses could be played with the following rhythm.

"Re- || *joice! Rejoice! Christ* | *is in you...* |

1 2 3 4 | 1 2 3 4

D G | D G D

> > | > > | *etc*

The rhythm of the verses (or one of the verses) could change to:

|| *"Now is the* | *time for us to* | *..."*

1 2 3 4 | 1 2 3 4

A

> | > |

19. Reading Scripture as the congregation hum the tune

A passage of Scripture can almost be given a new dimension when read to musical accompaniment. To enhance the effect even further, you could direct the people to *hum* the tune softly.

Example 37: When I feel the touch (SOF no.600)

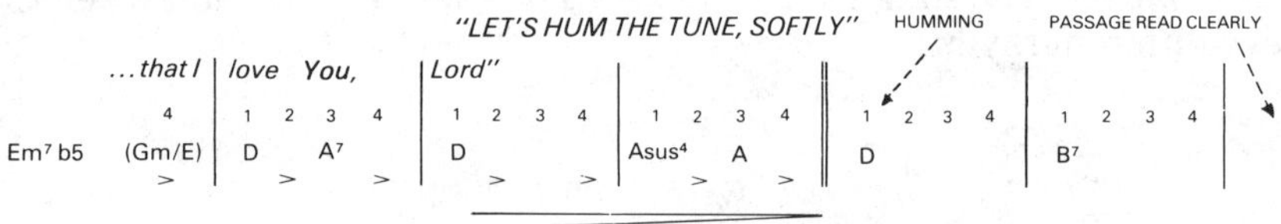

Main points

(a) Choose a passage of Scripture which matches the mood of the song you've been singing. For example, Psalm 139:13–18 shows how God, in creating each one of us, was expressing something in this universe which couldn't be expressed in any other way. We are a unique message from and about God which no one can duplicate. An ideal song to play before this passage of Scripture is read would be *Jesus, take me as I am* (SOF no.292).

(b) Make sure the musicians play softly, otherwise they will swamp both the humming and the reading.

(c) The passage of Scripture must be read slowly and clearly. If you are going to read while playing your guitar, then practise this!

(d) Don't use too lengthy a reading.

(e) At the appropriate place, bring the singing back in. This will mean saying, 'When I feel the touch,' to signal to people that this time through they will be required to sing rather than hum.

20. Singing Scripture to a variation of the song melody

Example 38: One of the times through a song, instead of reading Scripture, you could sing it (as the other musicians continue to play sensitively).
Main points:

(a) A good singing voice is required.

(b) The basic melody will have to be altered drastically in order for you to fit the words in.

(c) It is best if the reading begins when the tune begins, otherwise the sung reading will come halfway through the melody. This will sound odd. Therefore, as the previous verse is drawing to a close, pick up your Bible (already opened at the passage) and get ready to sing the Scripture as the tune begins.

(d) Practise spontaneously singing Scripture (e.g. the Psalms).

21. Reading or singing Scripture at the end of a song

Example 39: (a) Song (key of G) ends; (b) Musicians continue to play softly over a chord of G, or they play a sequence (a few chords repeated), for example: G(9)—G, Em(9)—Em, C(9)—C, Dsus4—D; (c) Scripture is read or sung against this backcloth.

Note: The instruments should compliment and emphasize the meaning of the words spoken. (This needs much practice.)

22. Repeating sections of songs

Some songs appear to have two main sections. Having sung the song through a couple of times, instead of singing it a third time, direct people to go back and sing the second section (usually the chorus section).

Note: This will need clear and confident direction.

Example 40: To illustrate this, here is the end of the second time through the song *I wiill sing unto the Lord* (SOF no.267), with a repeat of the second section.

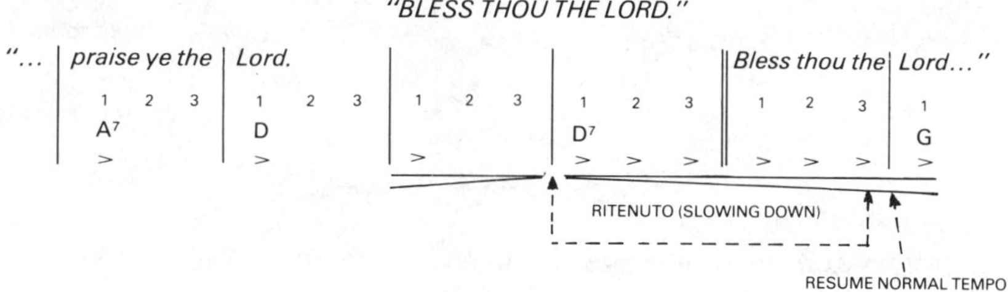

23. Singing only a section of a song

As one song finishes, it may be fitting at times not to sing the whole of another song but just a part of it. For example, imagine the song *Jesus we enthrone You* has just finished. In the silence that follows you might start singing (with accompaniment or without) the 'so exalt' section from the song *Majesty*. (The congregation will hopefully join you.)

24. Linking songs together

Part of the role of a worship leader is to make everything flow as smoothly as possible. Usually when a song finishes, it may be followed by a momentary pause, the title of the next song being announced, a brief comment about this next song, the instrumental introduction setting the tempo of the song and lastly the congregation joining in.

Technical hitches. Sometimes the points above don't flow in the way we had hoped. Some possible reasons for this are:

(a) A brief comment, intended as an aid to thoughtful worship, snowballs into a lengthy series of 'blessed thoughts'. This can easily happen if the leader is: (i) nervous, (ii) feeling the people should be responding better, or (iii) insufficiently prepared.

(b) There is an awkward hesitation between the end of the verbal introduction to the next song and the instrumental introduction, due to the lead musician being unsure about what to play as an introduction.

(c) The leader makes a few inspiring comments about the next song, but just as he is about to play the introduction, he realizes his capo is not affixed in the correct place. (Make sure capos are changed *as soon as one song finishes and before the verbal introduction to the next song*, otherwise it will take the edge off any illuminating thought-starters.)

Solution: One method of overcoming the snags we've been looking at is to link songs together.

Example 41: To illustrate this, here is the end of the song *I will enter His gates* (SOF no.252) linked to the song *For I'm building a people of power* (SOF no.109).

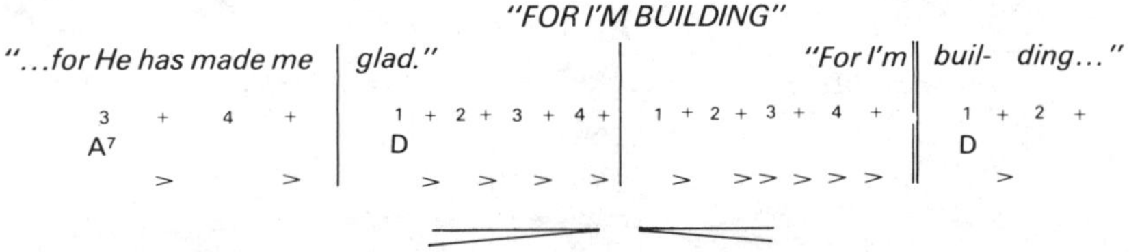

"FOR I'M BUILDING"

"...for He has made me	*glad."*	*"For I'm*	*buil- ding..."*
3 + 4 +	1 + 2 + 3 + 4 +	1 + 2 + 3 + 4 +	1 + 2 +
A^7	D		D
> >	> > > >	> >> > > >	>

(Other examples: SOF nos.337 to 604, 131 to 260, 92 to 71, 534 to 149, 358 to 630, 6 to 203, 18 to 136, 189 to 582.)

Look at the diagram in this previous example. In order for this technique to be carried out smoothly, you will have to:

(a) Tell the congregation what is about to happen. (This isn't necessary in situations where they are used to the idea already.) For instance, you could say something like this: 'We're going to begin our time together by singing the song *I will enter His gates*. Having sung it a number of times, we'll move straight on to sing *For I'm building a people of power*.' (If you say you're going to sing it *a number of times*, then if it feels right, you can carry on for a third time before moving on to the second song.) Make sure your instructions at the beginning are brief, uncomplicated and relaxed.

If they're not, people will have their minds more on getting the format right than on worshipping God.

(b) Announce *very clearly* the title of the new song in the gap between the two songs so that people don't carry on singing the first song.

(c) Drop the volume of the instrument(s) as you make this announcement, otherwise the music may muffle your directions.

(d) Raise the volume of the instruments(s) again afterwards.
(e) Increase the accents on the instruments(s) as you raise the volume.
(f) Sing the first phrase with confidence.

What songs are best linked together? Songs in the same: (a) tempo, (b) key, (c) theme, (d) mood. All four aspects don't *have* to be common to both songs, but at least aim for a few of these characteristics being present.

(a) *Tempo*: In the book and cassette *Teach Yourself Praise Guitar,* I showed that most songs you will come across fall happily into one of seven categories. Each of these groups can be played with one particular strumming pattern. Any two songs from any one of these groups can be joined together, bearing in mind that the songs should be related thematically, to some extent.

(b) *Key*: You may come across two songs which would link together very well thematically, but unfortunately they are not in the same key. Laying aside the issue of key changes between songs, which we will look at later, how do we tackle this problem?

Change the key of one or both songs, so that they are both in the same key. For example, the song *Lord, You are more precious* (SOF no.349) is in the key of G. The song *I just want to praise You* (SOF no.199) is in the key of F (capo 3 in D). The easiest thing to do here is to raise the second song into the key of G, so that both songs are in G. You have to be careful when doing this, keeping in mind the *highest* and *lowest* notes of the melodies of both songs. If you don't take this factor into consideration, you could end up with the situation where people have to be equipped with special breathing apparatus in order to scale the heights or plumb the depths of these new melodic ranges!

Rough guidelines for vocal ranges in songs: (1) Up-tempo songs C to E (2) Slow songs B to C (just over one octave).

Note: Whether people are sitting or standing as they sing can also have a bearing on these suggested ranges.

(c) *Theme*: Don't join two songs together just because they are in the same tempo and key. Ask yourself, 'What do we want to say to God at this point in our worship?' Then ask, 'What songs will express that best?'

(d) *Mood*: Though the songs *For this purpose* (SOF no.110) and *Open our eyes, Lord* (SOF no.420) are in the same tempo and key, the startling contrast in mood would unsettle any normal flow in worship.

25. Moving back and forth between two songs

Generally speaking, this works best with shorter songs, such as *Open our eyes, Lord*.

1st song – – – →	2nd song – – – →	1st song
(played a number of times)	(played a number of times using variations)	(maybe once only)

The role of leading worship is that of an enabler—helping people to be less aware of themselves and more aware of God. Using songs to create an uninterrupted block time of singing can help to achieve this. The following two examples deal with the mechanics of bridging songs smoothly so that the congregation is not distracted from the purpose of worshipping.

Example 42: Jesus, Name above all names (SOF no.288), *Open our eyes, Lord* (SOF no.420). (Capo 4 on cassette.)

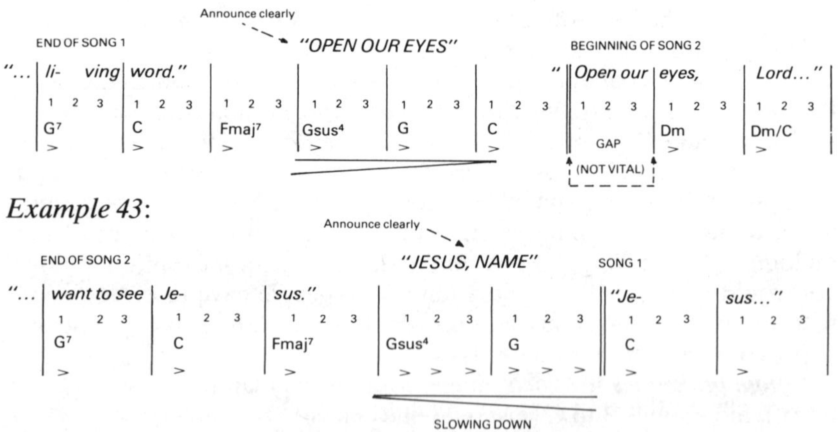

Example 43:

Here is a suggested running order of how you might combine these two songs. (*Don't* plan it out *beforehand*. Let it be a spontaneous response to the people's worship.)

Jesus, Name above all names	—together
Jesus, Name above all names	—Just the ladies (up to 'Emmanuel')
Jesus, Name above all names	—Just the men (from 'Emmanuel')
Open our eyes, Lord	—together
Open our eyes, Lord	—change words: 'Open *my* eyes...'
Open our eyes, Lord	—just the musicians
Jesus, Name above all names	—together (loudly)

Note: (a) *Ritenuto* (slowing down) could be employed effectively here as you announce that this is the last time through the song.

(b) The musicians need to agree on which chords are going to be played in the sections linking both songs.

26. Modulating (changing key) in the same song

This usually involves moving up into a new key. Look at the following example. Having played a few verses of the song in C major, we want to play the next verse in D major. Instead of suddenly leaping from one key to another, we can use either: (a) *one* modulating chord or (b) *two* modulating chords (see bar 3).

Example 44: *In my life, Lord* (Capo 3 in C, SOF no.216).

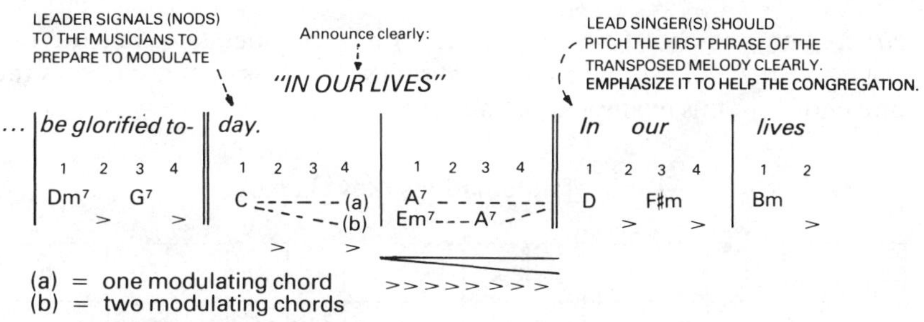

Note: (i) Make modulating very clear. Raise the volume at this point.

(ii) Take a firm lead in, singing the beginning of the melody in the new key.

(a) Rule for the use of one modulating chord.

This is always the chord on the *5th* note of the scale of the new key—in this example, the key of D major.

(Scale of new key of D)

D	E	F♯	G	A	B	C♯	D
1	2	3	4	5	6	7	8

MODULATION CHORD (A^7)

Note: Modulation chords tend to be '7th' chords. In the example above this means that A becomes A7. The addition of a '7th' to the plain chord gives the chord a feeling of incompletion, of being half-way to its goal. It is therefore an ideal chord to use as a 'stepping stone' to a new key.

(b) Rule for the use of two modulating chords.
In conjunction with the chord described in (a) we can use a minor 7th chord on the 2nd note of the scale of the new key.

(Scale of new key of D)

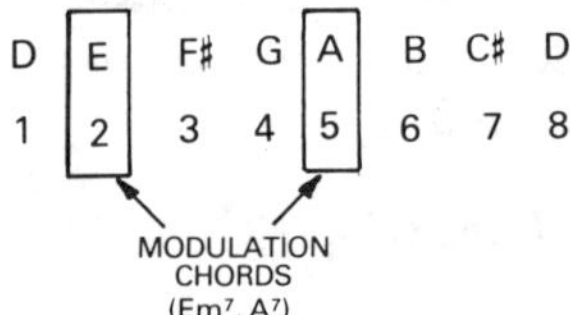

Note: The one-chord modulation (A7) is quite adequate, but the two chords (Em7, A7) sound richer. These last for the same duration as the one chord (in this example, just one bar).

Table of modulations (key changes)

NEW KEY (MAJOR OR MINOR)		A	B♭	B	C	D♭	D	E♭	E	F	F♯	G	A♭
MODULATION CHORDS	IIm^7	Bm^7	Cm^7	C♯m^7	Dm^7	E♭m^7	Em^7	Fm^7	F♯m^7	Gm^7	G♯m^7	Am^7	B♭m^7
	V^7	E^7	F^7	F♯^{7}	G^7	A♭^{7}	A^7	B♭^{7}	B^7	C^7	C♯^{7}	D^7	E♭^{7}

How to use the table

Let's imagine you were playing a song in the key of G major. If you wanted to go into the new key of A major, then you would look along the top line until you came to the letter A. The modulation chords necessary to get you into this new key are directly under this letter. In this case, the chords are Bm7 and E7. You could use both these chords or just E7. So your chord progression would look like this:

(a) G ⟶ E^7 ⟶ A; or (b) G ⟶ Bm^7 ⟶ E^7 ⟶ A

27. Singing counter-melodies (with the same words as the main tune)

Here the basic melody of the song is embroidered with an imitative melody. In order for this to be carried out successfully, one vocalist in the group leading the worship must continue to lead the congregation, while other vocalists (and even instrumentalists) introduce the answering phrase.

Example 45: *For I'm building a people of power* (SOF no.109).

Example: *He is Lord* (SOF no.159)

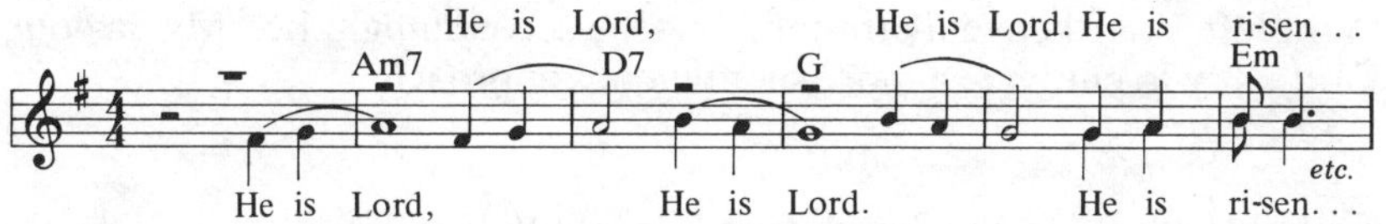

Example: *In my life, Lord* (SOF no.216)

28. Singing counter-melodies (to 'ooh', 'la', or to new words)

(a) *'Ooh'*. ('Ooh' fits better than 'la' in the following examples because of the mood of the songs.

Example 46: *Within the veil* (SOF no.616).

(b) *New words*. Experiment by making up your own words, either pre-planned or spontaneously.

Example 47: *Emmanuel* (SOF no.79).

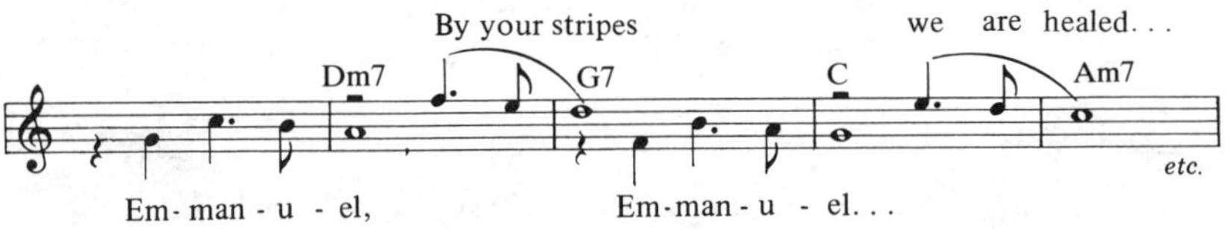

In the above example I have used a phrase containing three syllables each time. Don't be restricted to such an approach. Your first phrase might be, 'You left Your heavenly throne,' but the second might be, 'My Saviour God.' Try to cultivate a more spontaneous approach.

(c) *'La'*

Example 48: *When the Spirit of the Lord* (SOF no.604).
After having sung the various verses of this song ('sing', 'clap', 'praise' and 'dance'), direct the congregation to sing the melody to 'la'. After having done this, direct them to return to the original verses by announcing, 'I will *sing*,' etc. (in the gap between the verses). As people come to the chorus section of each verse, you could sing a counter-melody to 'la',

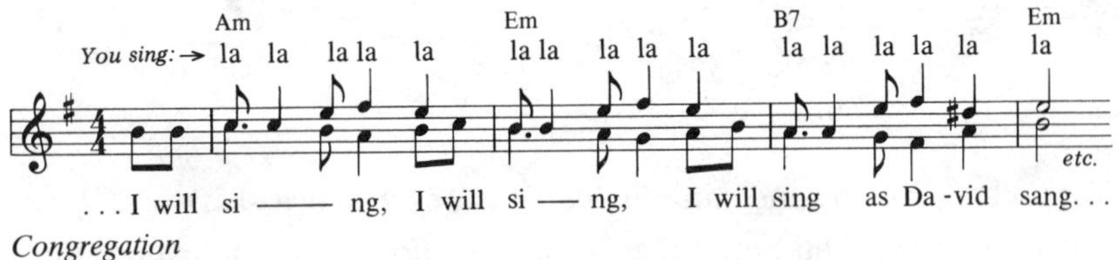

29. Extended codas (tailpieces)

The last few bars of a song can be used to act as a framework for improvised worship.

Example: *We are marching (Graham Kendrick Songbook).*

ever further and	‖: *dee- per*	*into the heart of*	| *God,*	*ever further and* :‖
D D/F♯	G	A⁷	D	D/F♯
3 4	1 2	3 4	1 2	3 4
>	>	>	>	>

Example 49: *Jesus how lovely You are* (SOF no.274).
Repeat the last chorus. Instead of singing the usual tune and words, introduce a new simple melody to 'ah', 'ooh' or 'la'. Most people will at

first continue to sing the usual tune or words, but some will follow you and launch out into this uncharted territory. Once some people seem to be picking up that new melody, introduce another. Note, it is *not* important that people follow the correct notes. You are essentially encouraging them to introduce their own vocal expression. As you continue to repeat the eight bars of the chorus, the vocal expression may develop into singing in tongues using fragments of these melodies you are introducing. Here are some suggestions for vocal melodies you might use.

Instead of singing these repeated melodies to 'ah', 'ooh' or 'la' you might find that you are able to fit the words of the song to the melodies with a little adjusting of the melody.

Example 50: *Jesus, how lovely You are* (SOF no.274). Here is the first melody slightly changed to accommodate the words.

Here is the third melody, again slightly altered to fit into the meter of the words.

Example 51: *We have come into this place* (SOF no.581).

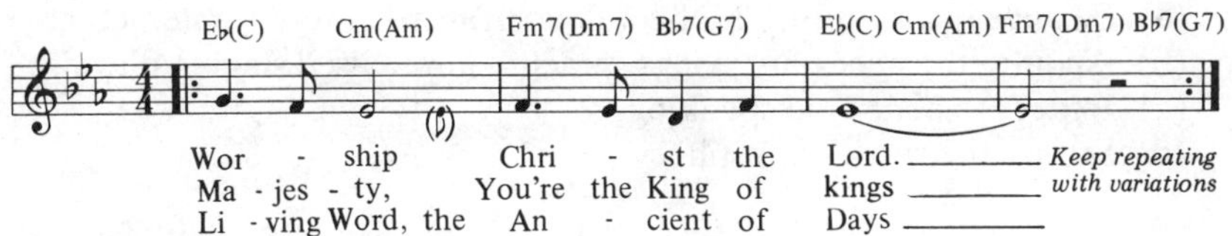

13

Prophetic Worship

Before we can break into new areas, we must first have a command of the basics. All the time our minds are preoccupied with capo placements and song numbers, it is less likely that we will be alert to the promptings of the Holy Spirit telling us to bring a spontaneous message from the Lord. What appears to be the unknown will remain so as long as we lack confidence in the fundemental techniques.

Be spiritually sensitive and develop the skills.

A prophet is a spokesman, an interpreter who speaks on behalf of another (Ex 4:15–16; 7:1). Prophecy is the word of God being given to us, but in order for this ministry to be effective it needs to be developed. Samuel and Elisha were both tutors of prophets. Men and women were instructed in the Scriptures, Jewish history and music. Chanting poems, proverbs, parables, history and genealogies were all part of this teaching.

The basis of this teaching has not changed.

(a) Be alive in the Spirit. Prophecy flows from a day-to-day interaction.
(b) Acquire the necessary skills—practise improvised singing/playing.
(c) Expect to hear God speaking.
(d) Stir up the spirit of prophecy.

(Ex 15:1–21; Judg 5:1–12; 1 Chron 25:1–3, 5; 2 Chron 20:14–17; 29:30.)

The term 'prophetic song', 'song to the Lord' (2 Chron 29:27) and 'spiritual song' are all interchangeable.

Maintaining the anointing

Many of the Old Testament leaders and prophets would have sung their prophecies. For example, Jahaziel's prophecy in 2 Chronicles 20:14 would probably have been sung. He was a Levite of the sons of Asaph, which meant he was trained as a musician. It is considered that as these musicians lived in daily repentance, they were always ready and prepared to prophesy should the king request it (1 Chron 25:2).

Unless we are continually abiding in Christ, we can't expect suddenly to bear the fruit of this ministry in a meeting. In Colossians 3:16, the prerequisite for singing prophetically is that we 'let the words of Christ dwell in [us] richly'. The power of the song will be proportional to the depth of our relationship with God. Just as evangelists should be ready to evangelize, counsellors to counsel and administrators to administrate, so should the musician be able at all times to maintain and flow in the prophetic anointing. Singers are very often reluctant to sing prophetically because they think simple statements of faith and truth are insufficient. The danger of waiting for more supposedly profound and significant words is that we end up wanting to impress the people.

Acquiring the skills

The levitical singers were taught how to sing prophetic songs (1 Chron 25:7). Their teacher was Chenaniah (1 Chron 15:22). If even *they* needed instruction on how to sing 'spontaneously' it would be presumptuous of us to think that we could sing in this way without mastering the necessary skills.

If the congregation is hindered from concentrating on the words of a prophecy because it is sung badly, it would be best simply to speak it, because the content of a message is more important than the way it is presented. The potential influence of a prophecy will be weakened if the singing is off-key or marred by the singer's nervousness. Singing prophetically in a meeting is very different from singing for pleasure. Even a good singer needs to develop techniques for this.

For practice—the elements of music (see exercises at back of book)

The same principles apply to both singers and instrumentalists. Unless we can operate confidently and fluently in a practice environment, we'll be unable to do so in a meeting.

Melody: Don't sing/play like Johnny one-note! Use intervals as well as moving by step. Give shape to the melodic line. Vary the types of tunes you use.

Range: Don't reach for notes out of your strongest range.

Harmony: When singing/playing to more than one chord, adjust the tune so that it relates to the chords. Don't sing/play regardless of the harmonic sense.

Phrasing: Use short musical sentences. Fit the phrases so that they sit comfortably into the chord progression. Don't be afraid to pause between each division, though don't wait too long.

Expression: Don't sing/play monotone. Adjust the tone quality. Contrast the levels of volume. Vary the intensity of notes.

Volume: Project your voice/playing. Because of nerves, even the best of singers seem to become inaudible when singing spontaneously.

Rhythm: Accentuate significant words/notes in a phrase.

Words: Convey your ideas with simplicity. People don't necessarily need to be hearing something which is *new*, but *true*. Learn to abbreviate concepts. Use imagery.

When leading exercises

* Let the group know who is playing/singing after whom. Unnecessary time is likely to elapse between each go if it is done at random.

* Emphasize that people should sing/play clearly and with strength, especially 'first-timers'.

* Encourage a go-for-it mentality.

* Don't be afraid to get people to repeat what they've just played/sung, particularly if their first attempt was feeble. Having broken the 'embarrassment barrier', it may be just what they want.

* Liberally affirm people's efforts after each go. This will increase confidence among the group.

If the exercise is dragging on, cut it short. The people who haven't played/sung can be the first to start the next exercise.

PROPHETIC PLAYING

The mind can sometimes fail to receive the word of God, possibly because of lack of faith, restrictions of the understanding, interpretation, prejudice or emotional defences due to hurts. Music is the language which God can use to reach deeper levels of our human make-up when the mind might not otherwise be receptive. As in 'programme music' (music with a story e.g. Peer Gynt by Grieg or Scheherezade by Rimsky Korsakov), where the instruments almost narrate the plot by 'painting' musical pictures, prophetic playing is a portrayal of what we feel God is saying to the people, using instruments. In one church, a leader told me that the previous Sunday their drummer had prophesied. Not thinking, I asked, 'What did he say?' The minister replied, 'Nothing. He simply played, and as he did so, people began to weep as God spoke powerfully through the anointing on the music.'

Prophetic playing is not the tune of a particular song emerging from a quieter pause in the meeting. This may be valid and appropriate but prophetic playing is something quite different. When you start, you are not sure what you are going to play! This sounds like a blind leap into the dark, but just as a spoken prophecy would issue from a life soaked in God and his word, so also would prophetic music be the outcome of daily worship, during which the instrumentalist would sometimes improvise. This spontaneous approach to private worship prepares the player to respond quickly to a cue from the Spirit in the meeting.

When the Lord compels you to play in this way, you'll naturally become keenly aware of the delicacy of the situation. You could easily get your fingers in knots—and wrong notes are not something you can keep to yourself! As you begin to play, you'll be asking yourself, 'Is this in the Spirit or in the flesh?' (or to de-jargonize it, 'Is this right or is this wrong?'). It might encourage you to realize that when Peter stepped out onto the water, all 'the flesh' were sitting in the boat!

When we step out in God, something of our self dies. Very often, the main thing which hinders us from exercising such faith is our reputation. Unfortunately, God is not interested in our reputation! Peter, for all his impetuosity, was not concerned with what people thought about him at that particular moment.

God enables those he calls

This is our source of encouragement to step out onto the spiritual tightrope. It may be far more comfortable to rely on our 'safety nets', 'harnesses' and 'handrails', but when we allow God to stretch us beyond what *we* can easily do, it's out there that he can bless most. When we have a set piece, we are confident on those grounds. Much of what happens in a meeting can be done without going beyond the boundaries of our own abilities. God's power, though, is to be found in the realm beyond ourselves.

Instrumental prophecy in Scripture

1. Music appears to stimulate the prophetic word. In 2 Kings 3:15, Elisha was only able to prophesy after a musician had ministered to him.

2. Prophetic music can lift our burdens and soothe us. In 1 Samuel 16:23, the evil spirit causing Saul's oppression recognized the powerful prophetic anointing on David's playing, and departed.

3. In 1 Chronicles 25:1–3, the levitical musicians were ready to prophesy at the order of the king.

4. Music can unfold the word of God to us: 'I will solve my riddle to the music of the lyre' (Ps 49:4).

5. There can be praise without words (Ps 150:3–5). The musician uses a musical vocabularly to speak to God.

Ways of prophesying with instruments

1. Playing after corporate singing.
2. Playing after a prophecy—to reiterate the message in another form.
3. Playing during a prophetic song—to underline any important words or phrases.

Note: As one instrument leads out, others should be prepared to accompany.

14

Singing in Tongues

'I will sing with the spirit and I will also sing with the mind' (1 Cor 14:15). Singing with the spirit means allowing the Holy Spirit not only to guide our speech, but the tune as well. It is impossible to tell you exactly *how* to speak or sing in tongues. Rather like learning to swim, the mechanics can be explained but the moment must come when your feet leave the security of the floor of the pool and your body relies on the buoyancy of the water. The psychological battle between yielding to fears and depending on the trustworthiness of the instructor must be fought and won. Many have settled down to accepting that God doesn't want them to have the gift of tongues. Yet no one would dream of saying, 'I give in, I can't swim,' before even trying to take their first few tentative strokes and splashes in the pool. Let's imagine that swimming is a spiritual gift. To find out whether or not you have this gift, what do you have to do? That's right, you'll never know—unless you *have a go!*

First steps

When we sing in tongues, it is *we* who are moving our tongues. God does not 'take us over'. It therefore follows that unless *we* begin to move our tongues and attempt to form some words, nothing will happen. No audible sounds will emerge from a mouth which is closed tight! God can't help you into this new praise language if the words you form are those of your native tongue. It is impossible to sing in two languages simultaneously! Your mind may want to use words you are familiar with but you have to trust the Holy Spirit to guide your voice to express what he wants you to express. So it is you speaking, but the Spirit provides the words.

Obstacles

People who find difficulty in being able to get started in this new language should not be put off by their inhibitions. They must persist. The feelings of uncertainty and embarrassment which can begin to assert themselves at the outset, can be due to all kinds of deep-rooted reasons:

Spiritual background

Each one of us is the result of our church environment. If our fellowship does not openly encourage the practice of tongues, then we are likely to be hesitant about using this gift. Faith breeds faith and unbelief breeds unbelief.

The suspicion of simpleness

The complexity of adulthood can make us so sophisticated that we are in danger of unnecessarily complicating the child-like faith with which we should approach the things of the Spirit. It is a sad state to get to when, in order to protect our inhibitions, we begin to regard scepticism as next to godliness.

The protest of the intellect

The intellect doesn't understand this new language. It is naturally wary when told that the ability and necessity to comprehend needs to be laid aside. Yet a great intellectual like Paul was able to say, 'If I pray in a tongue . . . my mind is unfruitful' (1 Cor 14:14). This doesn't mean that your thought processes switch off. When you are speaking or singing in tongues, I would encourage you to be thinking about the Lord.

Fear of losing control

Some are over-cautious about wanting this gift because they feel they might find themselves speaking in tongues when they are in a shop or on a bus! 1 Corinthians 14:32 says, 'The spirits of prophets are subject to prophets.' God does not pressurize or incite us, he prompts and inspires us. He wants us to work in co-operation with him. Mark 16:20 says, 'The Lord worked *with* them and confirmed the message by the signs.'

Comparison with others

Some find they are instantaneously able to find fluency in this new language. Just because others need time to work things through, this doesn't make them any less holy. Immediacy is not a hallmark of spirituality.

Governed by the will

There is nothing in the Greek original which suggests that speaking or singing in tongues has anything to do with emotion. It is a mistake to think that warm 'furry' feelings can help you begin to sing in this way. It is also a misconception to believe that one should become excited or aroused when singing in tongues. The Holy Spirit can be hindered by frenzied emotions just as much as by an obstinate will or an over-cautious mind. As with all expressions of praise and worship, singing in tongues operates not from our *feelings*, but from our *wills*.

Guidelines for a leader

1. When singing with the spirit happens in a meeting where some of those present are unaware of the teaching about such manifestations, a brief explanation should be given at once.
2. When a number of people sing with the spirit, no interpretation is necessary. (Otherwise this could take hours!)
3. If a person is going to deliver a message in tongues, it can be spoken or sung. This also applies to interpretation.
4. Don't extend the length of the singing unnecessarily, but don't allow the length and dynamics to become predictable either. In some churches one can almost measure to the second the moment at which the singing will die out. (This may cause some people to feel inhibited.)
5. Those who can sing in this way sometimes don't participate because

they don't *feel* prompted by the Holy Spirit. All singing, whether in our native tongue or not, is governed by the *will*. We must not wait for the right atmosphere to be generated before we begin to sing.

6. Get the balance between taking the initiative in starting the singing off yourself and allowing it to emerge from the body of the congregation. In some churches, singing with the spirit is unlikely to occur unless the leader gives the people a nudge.

7. Risk experimentation. If there is no development (i.e. the same few sing at the same volume for the same length of time), don't be afraid to instruct the congregation as to the various possibilities open to them. (Perhaps workshops can be arranged where the fellowship can look afresh at how worship can become more creative in its expression.)

The following section looks at some possible ways of enriching our times of singing in tongues.

1. Singing in tongues—using the song melody

The words of the song don't have to be replaced syllable for syllable with the words of your praise language.

The tune of the song should be regarded as a guideline around which you improvise with as few or as many notes as you want.

The mechanics

After singing a song a number of times through, you may feel it is right to lead the people to sing it again. This time, instead of people using the words of the song to accompany the melody, you direct them to sing in tongues (it may be that no such direction is necessary because as you begin to sing this verse in tongues, people follow your lead). Should you feel it *would* help the congregation to give a direction, *make it very clear*. Something simple like, 'Singing the tune—with the spirit,' would suffice.

As the singing commences, your vocal lead must be clear but not overpowering. (There is no premium in volume.)

On occasions, I have sensed that people are just beginning to step out and sing in this way when the worship leader suddenly draws things to a close. Any exercise of faith will involve a momentary 'tug-of-war' between belief and doubt. Singing the tune twice through provides a lengthy enough framework which will enable people to step out and enjoy singing in this way.

After singing the tune in tongues, you could direct people to return to singing the tune for the last time through, this time in their native tongue. If that is so, then simply make an announcement such as, 'In my life, last time.'

Alternatively, having sung the melody in tongues once or twice, you might draw the song to a close at that point.

A further option, after the tune has been sung in tongues, is to allow it to carry on without any main melody or accompaniment from the musicians.

Note: In each of the alternatives above, the worship leader must always be prepared to take a reliable lead.

2. Singing in tongues—at the end of a song

As the last chord of a song dies away, singing in tongues may occur. It may emerge from the body of the congregation or be started by the worship leader. If the musicians are to accompany the singing, they could (a) *play one chord without a definite rhythm.*

Guidelines on their use

As the singing in tongues begins, the musicians may wait for a few bars before playing quietly on the tonic chord (e.g. if the song is in the key of G major, the tonic chord is G).

Example 52: *Living under the shadow of His wing* (SOF no.331).

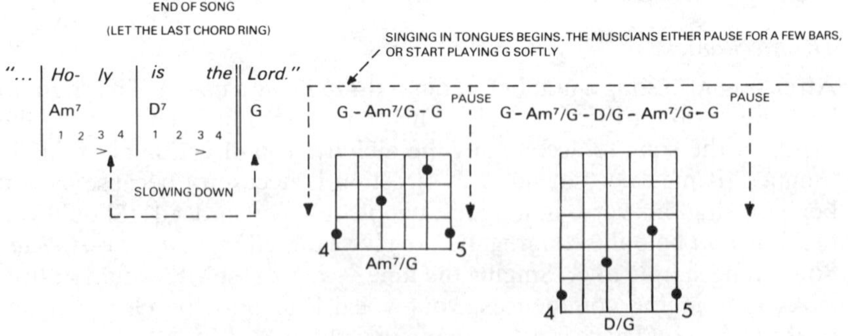

The root key of this singing is likely to be G, since the key of the song that has been sung is G.

As the singing in tongues continues, one guitar and piano can play the chord of G softly, while the other guitar plays the suggested chords. These moving chords of G—Am7/G—G will not clash with the basic root chord of G being played on the piano and other guitar *if the chords are played quickly, like passing chords, always returning to G*.

Example 53: As the musicians continue to improvise in G, the guitarist can use the following chords as alternatives to those in the above example.
Note: Emphasize the top/thinner strings.

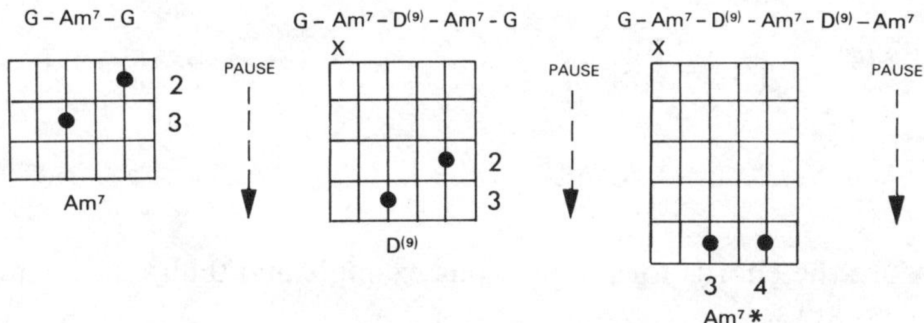

Example 54: Any combination of the chords in the previous example can be played like this:

Am7—G—Am7—G *pause* D(9)—Am7—D(9)—Am7—G—Am7—G

pause Am7*—D(9)—Am7*—D(9)—Am7—D(9)—Am7—G--Am7

—G *pause*

The best way of viewing this decorative chord work is to think of the guitarist's instrument as being equivalent to the vocalist's voice. Just as someone singing in tongues will shape a melody which rises and falls in its contour, so a guitarist is attempting to create similar peaks and troughs with these chords, moving back and forth to G.

(b) Another alternative is to *play one chord with a definite rhythm.*
Guidelines: As singing in tongues emerges, the musicians accompany with a rhythmic pattern (maybe the same as that of the song). This rhythm may begin softly, becoming more prominent by the use of regular accents.

Example 55: Here is the end of example 52, this time played rhythmically.

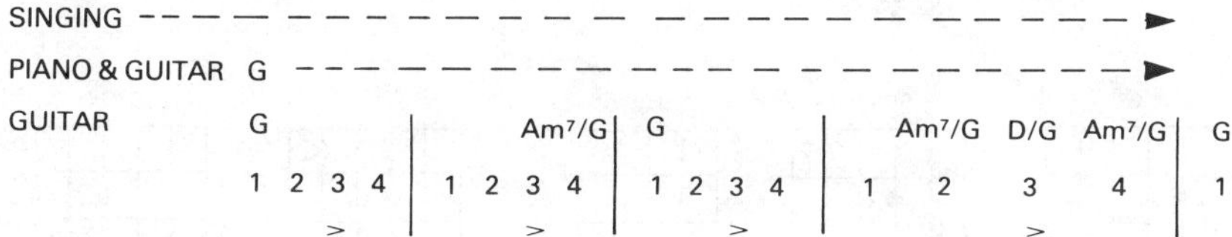

Example 56: To demonstrate this in another key, here is the end of the song *Ascribe greatness* (SOF no.18).

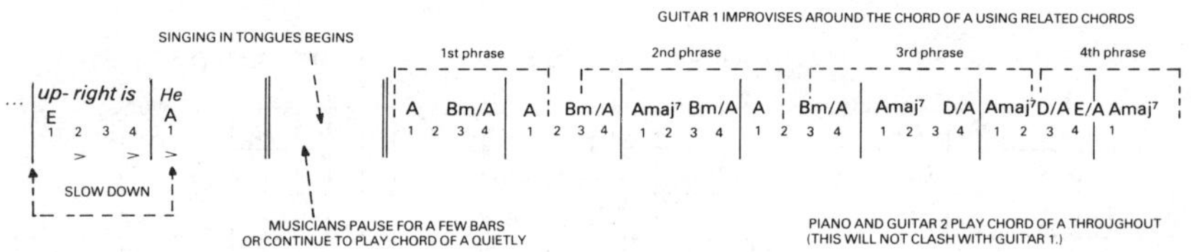

Below are the chords for the previous example and their equivalents in other easy keys.

Note: the circled numbers refer to the frets.

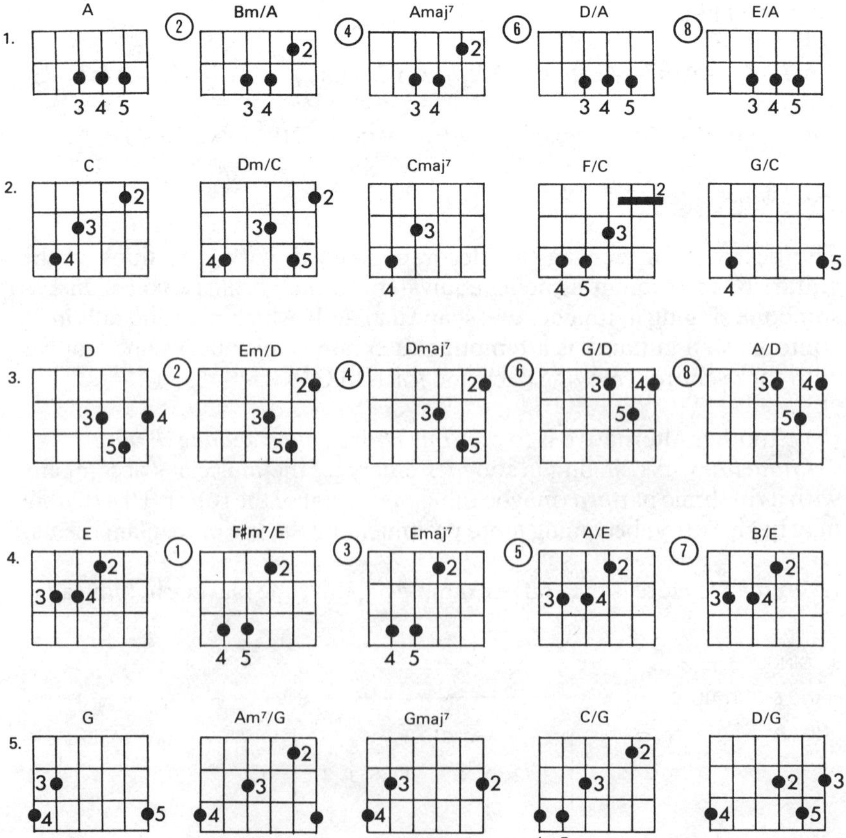

1.	A	② Bm/A	④ Amaj⁷	⑥ D/A	⑧ E/A
2.	C	Dm/C	Cmaj⁷	F/C	G/C
3.	D	② Em/D	④ Dmaj⁷	⑥ G/D	⑧ A/D
4.	E	① F♯m⁷/E	③ Emaj⁷	⑤ A/E	⑦ B/E
5.	G	Am⁷/G	Gmaj⁷	C/G	D/G

(c) You could *play a sequence (a few chords repeated) without a rhythm.* (See the table of chord sequences on pages 129–130 for further ideas.)

The repetitious nature of a sequence can provide a secure framework for people to sing in the Spirit. For many, launching out into a new language can be enough of a problem without having to compose melodies as well.

The musicians must be alert and sensitive to one another and to the congregation if they are to be quick in flowing together into such a move.

One musician must establish the chords in the sequential phrase. This is usually the lead musician.

For example:

‖: Gmaj^7 // | Cmaj^7 // | Am^7 // | D^7 // :‖

The other musicians must have identified the chords of the sequence before they begin to play, otherwise their uncertainty will be conveyed through their playing. It would be best, therefore, if they let the lead musician play the sequence a couple of times before they join in.

The musicians will need precise direction as they continue to play in this way. As well as attempting to worship, they will be looking to the worship leader and trying to gauge whether, for instance, they should be getting louder, softer, slowing down to stop or injecting more rhythm.

A congregation's ability to sing in tongues without being disturbed by the use of such chords is something which can only come with practice. Some fellowships seem to be able to sing spontaneously while the musicians use complicated chords to form sequences. In the main, however, keep your sequences *simple*.

(d) Alternatively, you could *play a sequence with a definite rhythm*. (See the table of chord sequences on pages 129–130 for further ideas.)

Example 57: *Emmanuel* (SOF no.79).

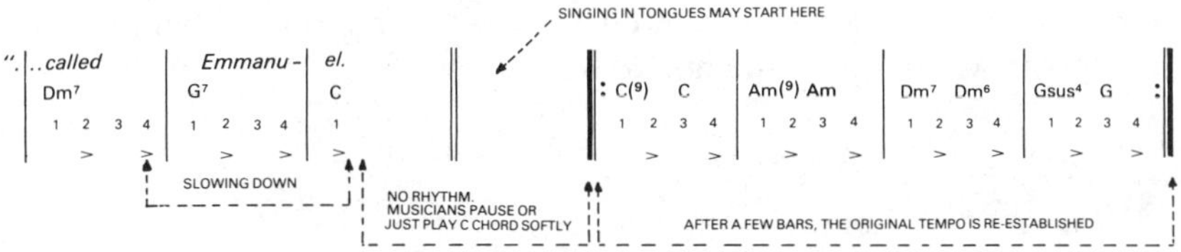

Guidelines: All points applying to sequences *without* a definite rhythm apply here too. Also, the lead musician must accentuate the rhythm so that the other musicians are not left in doubt.

All the above points in this section can be played in different ways to accompany the singing: (i) softly throughout, (ii) gradually growing in volume (crescendo) then dying away (decrescendo), (iii) crescendo, decrescendo, crescendo, decrescendo.

The musicians need to work at the 'chemistry' and sensitivity between them for these changes in dynamics to be smooth.

3. Singing in tongues—out of a time of quiet

Singing in tongues can be especially beautiful when started out of a period of stillness and silence in the meeting. As people are quiet, sensing the presence of God in their midst, you could say: 'Let's be quietly singing in tongues, focusing our minds on the Lord.' I have found this approach especially helpful in encouraging many to take their first tentative steps along what can appear to be a spiritual gang-plank.

Note: All the possibilities and various dynamic combinations in sections 1 and 2 can be used in this third section.

Worship or the worship of worship?

Obviously great attention needs to be paid to what is happening in the congregation when the suggestions in these sections are carried out. The musicians must be careful that they don't rush ahead and try to carry the congregation further than they are ready to go. If the musicians are concentrating on *serving* the congregation and the Lord with their music, it will help guard against the subtle, inconspicuous ways in which self-indulgence and ego-projecting can creep in to the worship. Worship which becomes 'gimmicky' will not set us free but will have quite the opposite effect. Just because there is an absence of liturgy and form doesn't mean worship is being produced. Often when the desire to worship is at its strongest, it is then that we need to make sure that it is being directed to God alone. When we are at our most creative in worship, self-gratification may well be close to the surface. Therefore, we need to *be* worshippers and not *do* worship.

15
Responsive Singing

This was a very common form of singing used in Israel. A phrase would be sung by one or more singers and repeated by others. This was either planned or spontaneous. There are different kinds of responsive singing used in Scripture.

(a) Leader to another singer (1 Sam 18:7; 21:11; 29:5; Is 6:3–4).
(b) Leader to a group of singers (Ex 15:21; Ps 44; 47; 99).
(c) One group to another group (Neh 12:31, 40, 42; Ez 3:11).
(d) Singers to instruments (Is 38:20).
(e) Leader to congregation (Ps 106; 107; 118; 136).

The repetition of an idea was supposed to reinforce it in the mind of the hearer. Listening and participation were both involved. Hence, it became a good teaching aid. This can be true today, where leader and congregation sing back and forth around a particular topic (e.g. the second coming of Christ). The main kinds of responses used are (a) imitation, (b) question and answer.

Example 58: Imitative response—leader to congregation.
As a song finishes, let it flow into a chord sequence. The leader then sings a phrase (related to the point you have arrived at in the worship). The congregation echoes this phrase. It is preferable that a gap is left between both phrases, as opposed to them overlapping, as in *I will call upon the Lord* (SOF no.251). To help the congregation to join in, the leader needs to say, 'Together,' after singing the first phrase.

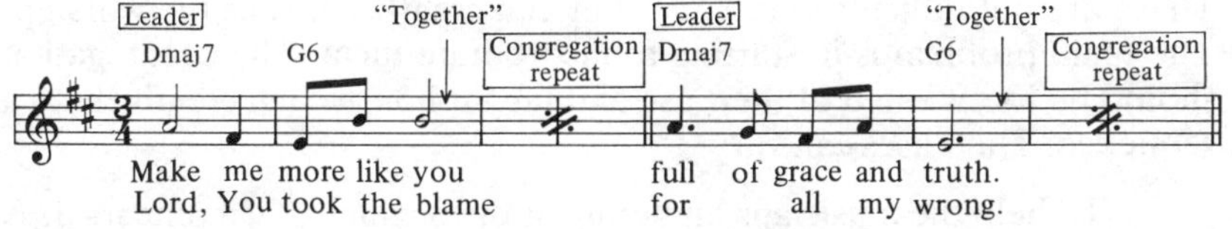

Also, the music group/choir should regard themselves as a smaller example of the congregation and lead the way strongly with the responsive singing.

The congregation will then hopefully follow their example. In order that the leader doesn't find himself singing without the response, the music group/choir need to be quick on the up-take. Any likely misunderstandings should be clarified during rehearsal.

Example 59:

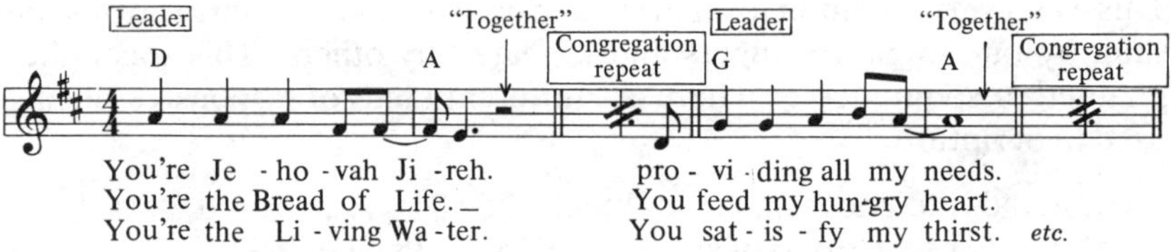

Exercise: Divide singers into groups of two. Give each group a theme, for example, the names of God, warfare, peace, joy, love, the character of God, repentance. Let them have five minutes to prepare how they are going to sing. Each group should be given a chord sequence to sing to as it would become monotonous if only one chord sequence was used for all the groups.

16

Chord Sequences

These are not difficult to use and they can greatly enhance the worship. The main problem is in starting to incorporate them. The congregation should be forewarned of their use and taught how to sing creatively to a sequence. Their uses can vary:

(a) To help the musicians limber up at the beginning of a rehearsal. A chord sequence can act as a framework for everyone to improvise to.

(b) At an appropriate point in the worship, the leader may direct the musicians to minister to the people or the Lord using a sequence (rather than starting from cold).

(c) To accompany singing in tongues, instead of just one chord being played. (See the section on *Singing in tongues,* p.118.)

(d) At the end of a song, the leader may encourage people to sing out the names of God or verses relating to the theme of the worship at that point, for example, repentance or God's holiness. A sequence can help to give this shape and form.

(e) During responsive singing. (See the section on *Responsive singing*, p.127.)

Note: A chord sequence must build on the mood of the worship.

Key: The letters in brackets in the left-hand column refer to keys for the guitarist. He will find these particularly interesting and also the chords on the asterisked lines. (These chords are all in the chord charts at the back.) Each chord should be a minim (two crotchets) in length.

Examples 60–76: On the cassette, all the asterisked and bracketed chords are played.

GUITAR KEYS	CHORDS				ROMAN NUMERAL EQUIVALENTS			
	C	F	C	F	I	IV	I	IV
(A,E,G)	C	F/C	C	F/C	I	IV/I	I	IV/I
(A,E)	C	Fm	C	Fm	I	IVm	I	IVm
(A,D,E)	C	Fm/C	C	Fm/C	I	IVm/I	I	IVm/I
	C	F	C	G	I	IV	I	V
	C	F/C	C	G/C	I	IV/I	I	V/I
	C	G	F	G	I	V	IV	V
(A,D,E)	C	G/C	F/C	G/C	I	V/I	IV/I	V/I
	C	Am	Dm^7	G	I	VIm	IIm^7	V
Example 60: (G)	*C$^{(9)}$C	Am$^{(9)}$Am	Dm^{7}Dm^6	G$^{(9)}$G	I$^{(9)}$I	VIm$^{(9)}$VIm	IIm^7 IIm^6	V$^{(9)}$V
	C	Am	F	G	I	VIm	IV	V
	C	B♭	C	B♭	I	♭VII	I	♭VII
	C	B♭	F	C	I	♭VII	IV	I
	C	B♭/C	F/C	G	I	♭VII/I	IV/I	V
	C	B♭	A♭	B♭	I	♭VII	♭VI	♭VII
	C	B♭	F/A	A♭	I	♭VII	IV/VI	♭VI
	C	B♭/C	F/C	A♭/E♭	I	♭VII/I	IV/I	♭VI/♭III
Example 61: (D)	C	B♭$^{(9)}$	F	F/G	I	♭VII$^{(9)}$	IV	IV/V
	C	E♭	F	C	I	♭III	IV	I
Example 62: (G)	C	E♭^{6}	F$^{(9)}$	C	I	♭III^6	IV$^{(9)}$	I
	C	E♭	F	A♭	I	♭III	IV	♭VI
	C	E♭/C	F/C	A♭/C	I	♭III/I	IV/I	♭VI/I
	C D/C	C	A♭ B♭/A♭	A♭	I II/I	I	♭VI ♭VII/♭VI	♭VI
	C	Em	F	G	I	III	IV	V
	C	Em^7	F	F/G	I	III^7	IV	IV/V
	C	F	Dm^7	G^7	I	IV	IIm^7	V^7
	C	Gm^7	C	Gm^7	I	Vm^7	I	Vm^7
Example 63: (A,D)	C	Gm^7	B♭maj^7	C	I	Vm^7	♭VIImaj^7	I
	Cmaj^7	Fmaj^7	Cmaj^7	Fmaj^7	Imaj^7	IVmaj^7	Imaj^7	IVmaj^7
Example 64: (A,D,E)	C	Dm/C	Cmaj^7	Dm/C	I	IIm^7/I	Imaj^7	IIm^7/C
Example 65:	*Cmaj^7	Bm$^{7(11)}$	E	Esus^4	Imaj^7	VIIm$^{7(11)}$	III	IIIsus^4
	C	Cmaj^7	Dm^7/C	Fm^6/C	I	Imaj^7	IIm^7/I	IVm^6/I
Example 66:	*C	Dm/C	G^7/C	C	I	IIm/I	V^7/I	I
Example 67:	*C	D/C	Dm$^{7♭5}$/C	C	I	II/I	IIm$^{7♭5}$/I	I
	C	A♭^{o}/C	C	A♭^{o}/C	I	♭VI°/I	I	♭VI°/I

GUITAR KEYS	CHORDS				ROMAN NUMERAL EQUIVALENTS			
	Am	G	F	E	Im	VII	VI	V
	Am	C	Dm	E	Im	III	IVm	V
	Am	C	D	F	Im	III	IV	VI
	Am	Dm^{7}	Am	E	Im	IV^{7}	I	V
	Am	Em^{7}	Am	Em^{7}	Im	V^{7}m	I	Vm^{7}
	Am	Em^{7}	Fmaj^{7}	G	Im	V^{7}m	VImaj^{7}	VII
Example 68: (Dm)	*Am	Am♯^{7}	Am^{7}	Am♯^{7}	Im	Im♯^{7}	I^{7}	Im♯^{7}
	Am	Am♯^{7}	Am^{7}	D^{9}	Im	Im♯^{7}	Im^{7}	IV^{9}
Example 69:* (Em)	Am$^{(9)}$	Am	Dm^{7}	Dm^{6}	Im$^{(9)}$	I	IVm^{7}	IVm^{6}
Example 70: (Dm)	*Am	Bm/A	C/A	Bm/A	Im	IIm/I	III/I	IIm/I
Example 71:	*Am$^{(9)}$	Bm$^{(11)}$	Cmaj^{7}	Bm^{7}sus^{4}	Im$^{(9)}$	IIm$^{7(11)}$	IIImaj^{7}	IIm^{7}sus^{4}
	Am	D/A	E^{7}/A	Am	Im	IV/I	V^{7}/I	Im
Example 72:* (Dm)	*Am	E/A	A^{7}sus^{4}	A^{7}	Im	V/I	I^{7}sus^{4}	I^{7}
	Am^{7}	D^{7}	Gmaj^{7}	Em^{7}	Im^{7}	IV^{7}	VIImaj^{7}	Vm^{7}
†*Example 73*:* (Em)	Am$^{(9)}$	F/A	G/A	Am	Im$^{(9)}$	VI/I	VII/I	Im
Example 74:	*Am	Dm^{7}	Gmaj^{7}	Cmaj^{7}	Im	IVm^{7}	VIImaj^{7}	IIImaj^{7}
(continued)	F♯m$^{7\flat5}$	B^{7}	Em	E^{7}	♯VIm$^{7\flat5}$	II^{7}	Vm	V^{7}
Example 75:	*Am	D^{7}	Gmaj^{7}	Cmaj^{7}	Im	IV^{7}	VIImaj^{7}	IIImaj^{7}
(continued)	F♯m$^{7\flat5}$	B^{7}	Em	E^{7}	♯VIm$^{7\sharp5}$	II^{7}	Vm	V^{7}
	Am	D^{7}/A	Gmaj^{7}	Cmaj^{7}/G	Im	IV^{7}/I	VIImaj^{7}	IIImaj$^{7\flat}$/VII
(continued)	F♯m$^{7\flat5}$	B^{7}/F♯	Em	E^{7}	♯VIm$^{7\flat5}$	II^{7}/♯VI	Vm	V^{7}
	Am	E^{7}/B	F/C	G/D	Im	V^{7}/II	VI/III	VII/IV
(continued)	Cmaj^{7}/E	Fmaj^{7}	D/F♯	E^{7}/G♯	IIImaj^{7}/V	VImaj^{7}	IV/♯VI	V^{7}/♯VII
Example 76:	*Dm^{7}	G^{7}	Cmaj^{7}	Fmaj^{7}	IVm^{7}	VII^{7}	IIImaj^{7}	VImaj^{7}
(continued)	Bm$^{7\flat5}$	E^{7}	Am	A^{7}	IIm$^{7\flat5}$	V^{7}	Im	I^{7}
	Fmaj^{7}	Bm$^{7\flat5}$	Em^{7}	Am^{7}	VImaj^{7}	IIm$^{7\flat5}$	Vm^{7}	Im^{7}
(continued)	Dm	Ab^{0}	Am	C^{7}	IV	♭I^{0}	Im	III^{7}
	Fmaj^{7}/E	D^{0}	Em^{7}/D	Am^{7}/C	VImaj^{7}/V	IV^{0}	Vm^{7}/IV	Im^{7}/III
(continued)	Dm^{7}/C	G^{7}/B	Cmaj^{7}/B	A^{7}	IVm^{7}/III	VII^{7}/II	IIImaj^{7}/II	I^{7}
	† No 3rd note in these chords							

Note: When using Roman numerals to locate chords in other keys apart from C and Am, this table will help you:

KEY ↓

I	II	III	IV	V	VI	VII
C	D	E	F	G	A	B
D♭	E♭	F	G♭	A♭	B♭	C
D	E	F♯	G	A	B	C♯
E♭	F	G	A♭	B♭	C	D
E	F♯	G♯	A	B	C♯	C♯
F	G	A	B♭	C	D	E
G♭	A♭	B♭	C	D♭	E♭	F
G	A	B	C	D	E	F♯
A♭	B♭	C	D♭	E♭	F	G♭
A	B	C♯	D	E	F♯	G♯
B♭	C	D	E♭	F	G	A
B	G♯	D♯	E	F♯	G♯	A♯

↑ KEY

17

Exercises for Singers and Musicians

Singers

Example

Each singer is given a verse from a Psalm. The musicians play a chord sequence (pp.129–130). The first singer sings the first verse, the second singer immediately sings the next verse, etc.

Aim: Melodic improvisation

Example

As above, but now putting the verses into your own words.

Aim: Paraphrasing Scripture. For example, 'Jesus, full of grace and truth.'

Example 77

(a) Ask the singers to write a four-line verse (it doesn't have to rhyme) summing up what they feel God is saying to them through the verse, 'The Lord's my Shepherd, I shall not want.' (E.g. 'I am the guide of all your ways; your future is in my hands. I cannot improve on my plan for your life.')

(b) The musicians play a chord sequence (e.g. Am(9)—Bm7sus4—Cmaj7).

(c) One by one, the singers sing what they've come up with.

Aim: Personalizing Scripture.

Example 78

Select a number of short passages (e.g. Acts 2:1–4; Eph 3:8–12; Col 1:15–20; Rev 4:8–11; 5:11–14; 7:9–12.) Musicians play a chord sequence and each singer sings their passage.

Aim: Rhythmic phrasing of words.

Example 79

Ask people to think of three to four names or titles given to God in Scripture. Musicians play a sequence (e.g. C—Dm/C—G7/C—C). One by one the singers sing their names (e.g. 'You are the Messiah, the Ancient of Days, the Lamb slain before the foundation of the world').

Aim: Knowledge and quick use of Scripture.

Example 80

(a) Singers are asked to sing their thoughts (or verses) around a theme which the leader sets (e.g. God's holiness).

(b) The musicians play a chord sequence (e.g. Em—G—A—C).

(c) After the first singer, the second sings, etc.

Aim: To develop biblical themes.

Example 81

Singers in pairs are given a theme (e.g. repentance, healing, etc.). The first singer sings one thought, then the second (a) repeats this as accurately as possible, (b) sings a contrasting tune, or (c) sings a contrasting idea.

Aim: Develops togetherness. Also, sometimes a prophetic song can be sung by one person with another joining in to add harmonies, echoing phrases, or even singing contrasting thoughts.

Musicians

Example

Guitars play a chord sequence. One by one the lead instruments (e.g. flute, piano) improvise using the *full range* of their instruments.

Aim: Improvisation, constructing interesting melodies.

Example

Guitars play a sequence. One lead instrument plays a phrase, another copies it.

Aim: Helps musicians listen and play off each other.

Example 82

Lead singer sings an improvised melody to 'la' over a sequence (e.g. Cmaj7—Bm7sus4—E—Esus4). Lead instruments complement the melody with answering phrases, etc.

Aim: In prophetic singing, instruments can dramatize what is being sung.

Example

Guitars play a sequence. The lead singer sings fragments of a melody to 'la'. The instruments play phrases which are (a) imitative (b) contrasting.

Aim: To develop pitch and listening.

CHORDS

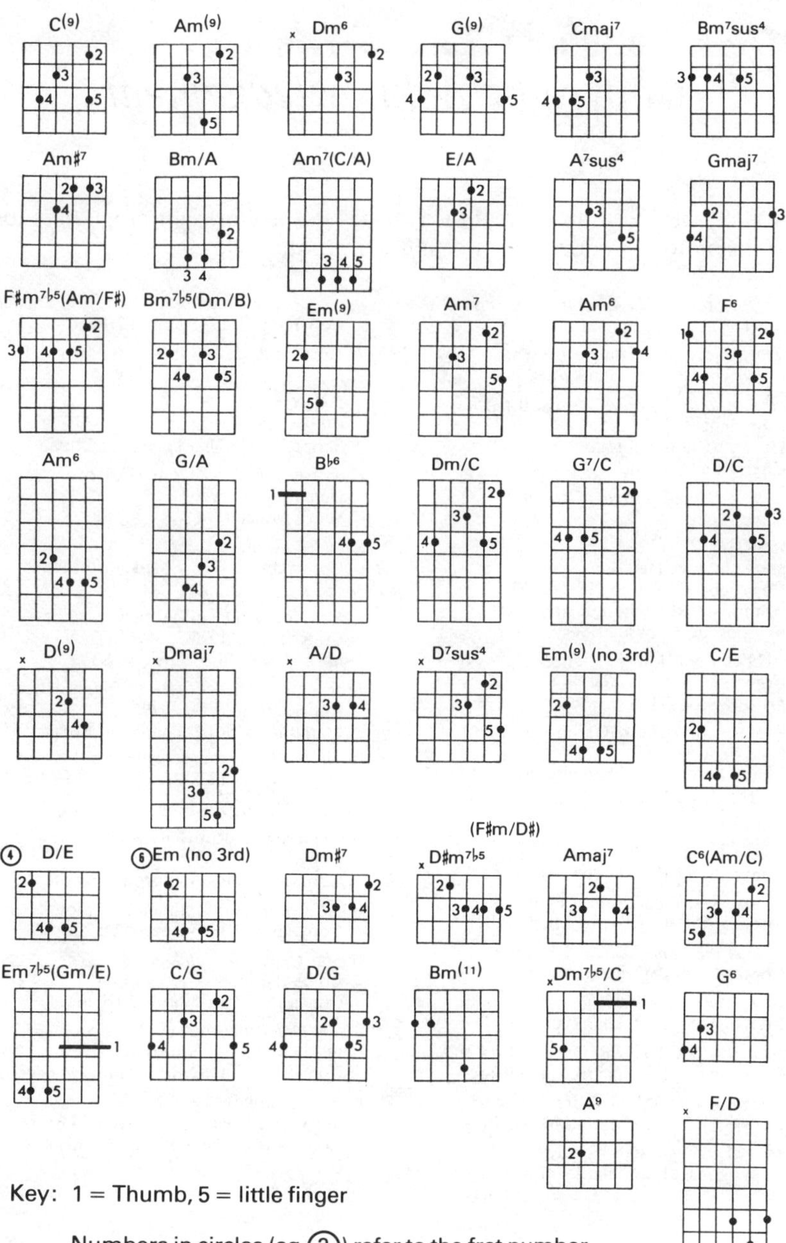

Key: 1 = Thumb, 5 = little finger

Numbers in circles (eg ②) refer to the fret number

Copyright Acknowledgement

The publishers wish to express their thanks to the copyright proprietors for permission to reproduce words or music from the following songs:

When the Spirit of the Lord is within my heart Author Unknown

River wash over me Dougie Brown
Copyright © 1980 Thankyou Music

I will sing unto the Lord Donya Brockway
Copyright © 1972
His Eye/Cherry Blossom/
Cherry Lane Music

For I'm building a people of power
Dave Richards
Copyright © 1977 Thankyou Music

Majesty Jack W Hayford
Copyright © 1976 Rocksmith Music
Administered in the UK and Eire
by Leosong Copyright Service

I love You Lord Laurie Klein
Copyright © 1978, 1980
Word Music (UK)

Holy is the Lord Kelly Green
Copyright © 1982
Mercy Publishing/Thankyou Music

Holy is the Lord of hosts Bruce Clewett
Copyright © 1983 Thankyou Music

Emmanuel Dave Fellingham
Copyright © 1985 Thankyou Music

Open our eyes, Lord Robert Cull
Copyright © 1976 Word Music (UK)

Worthy is the Lamb David J Hadden
Copyright © 1982 Restoration Music Ltd

God of glory Dave Fellingham
Copyright © 1982 Thankyou Music

Jesus how lovely You are Dave Bolton
Copyright © 1975 Thankyou Music

His name is wonderful Audrey Meir
Copyright © 1959 Manna Music Inc

Peace I give to you Graham Kendrick
Copyright © 1979 Thankyou Music

I will call upon the Lord Michael O'Shields
Copyright © 1981 Sound III Inc

Thank You Jesus Author Unknown

Hallelujah for the Lord our God
Dale Garratt
Copyright © 1972
Scripture in Song/Thankyou Music

Father we love You Donna Adkins
Copyright © 1976, 1981
Word Music (UK)

Rejoice! Graham Kendrick
Copyright © 1983 Thankyou Music

When I feel the touch
Keri Jones, Dave Matthews
Copyright © 1978
Springtide/Word Music (UK)

Jesus name above all names Naida Hearn
Copyright © 1974, 1979
Scripture in Song/Thankyou Music

In my life Lord Bob Kilpatrick
Copyright © 1978 Prism Tree Music

He is Lord Marvin Frey

Within the veil Ruth Dryden
Copyright © 1978
Genesis Music/Thankyou Music

We are marching Graham Kendrick
Copyright © 1985 Thankyou Music

We have come into this place
Bruce Ballinger
Copyright © 1976 Sound III Inc

Living under the shadow of His wing
David J Hadden and Bob Sylvester
Copyright © 1982 Restoration Music

Ascribe greatness
Mary Lou Locke and Mary Kirkbride
Copyright © Peter West

Teach Yourself PRAISE GUITAR

Book and Cassette

As many people are touched by the move of God's Spirit, there is an increasing desire to worship and to learn new songs. The guitarist has an important part to play in both large and small gatherings.

Jo King has for many years been helping people to play the guitar with enough confidence and skill to lead others in praise and worship. This book shows step by step how you can master the common chord shapes, and then how to apply seven strumming techniques so that your playing has variety and is always suited to the mood of each song.

Jo King is a concert evangelist and conducts 'worship workshops' throughout the country. He is also a member of the Scripture Union schools team.

- **An invaluable aid to beginners and more established guitarists alike.**
- **Practical – born out of many years' teaching experience.**
- **Fully illustrated for maximum clarity.**
- **Includes practical hints on how to lead others in praise and worship.**
- **The book and cassette are designed to be used in conjunction with each other and are fully cross-referenced. Together they form an invaluable teaching aid.**

Kingsway Publications

BOOK ISBN 0 86065 228 9
CASSETTE KMC 399

SONGS & HYMNS OF FELLOWSHIP

Price £15.95
Gift Edition with marker ribbon, gold edges and slipcase. **Price £19.95**

INTEGRATED MUSIC EDITION

The complete music from *Songs of Fellowship Bks 1, 2 & 3* and *Hymns of Fellowship* in one book.

★ 645 songs and hymns in one alphabetical order matching the *Integrated Words Edition.*
★ Fully scored for piano with guitar chords.
★ All 2-page songs on facing pages avoiding turnovers.
★ Full indexes of first lines, titles, scripture references and subject themes, plus complete chord charts.
★ Scripture references appear against each song and hymn where appropriate.
★ Cased bound in quality material and thread-sewn for security of binding.
★ Lightweight paper to reduce bulk for easy handling – this and thread-sewing allow pages to open as flat as possible.

INTEGRATED WORDS EDITION

No church should be without this mammoth collection of 645 songs and hymns for praise and worship.

★ Includes all the songs from *Songs of Fellowship Bks 1, 2 & 3* and *Hymns of Fellowship,* in one alphabetical order for easy use in praise and worship meetings.
★ With full index of titles and first lines, and index of Scripture references.
★ Cassettes are available for learning the songs.

Only £1.50

Order from your local Christian Bookshop, or in case of difficulty direct from:
The Rainbow Company, PO Box 77, Hailsham, E. Sussex BN27 3EF.

Songs of Fellowship Arrangement Service

Apart from the fully scored music editions, individual instrumental and vocal arrangements are available for most of the songs in the *Songs of Fellowship* range from:

The Songs of Fellowship Arrangement Service,
PO Box 4, Sheffield, South Yorkshire S1 1DU.

Please send an A4 stamped addressed envelope (100 grammes postage).